To my grandmother who was a real fairy in the kitchen and taught me the power of singing while cooking and the pure joy of experimentation

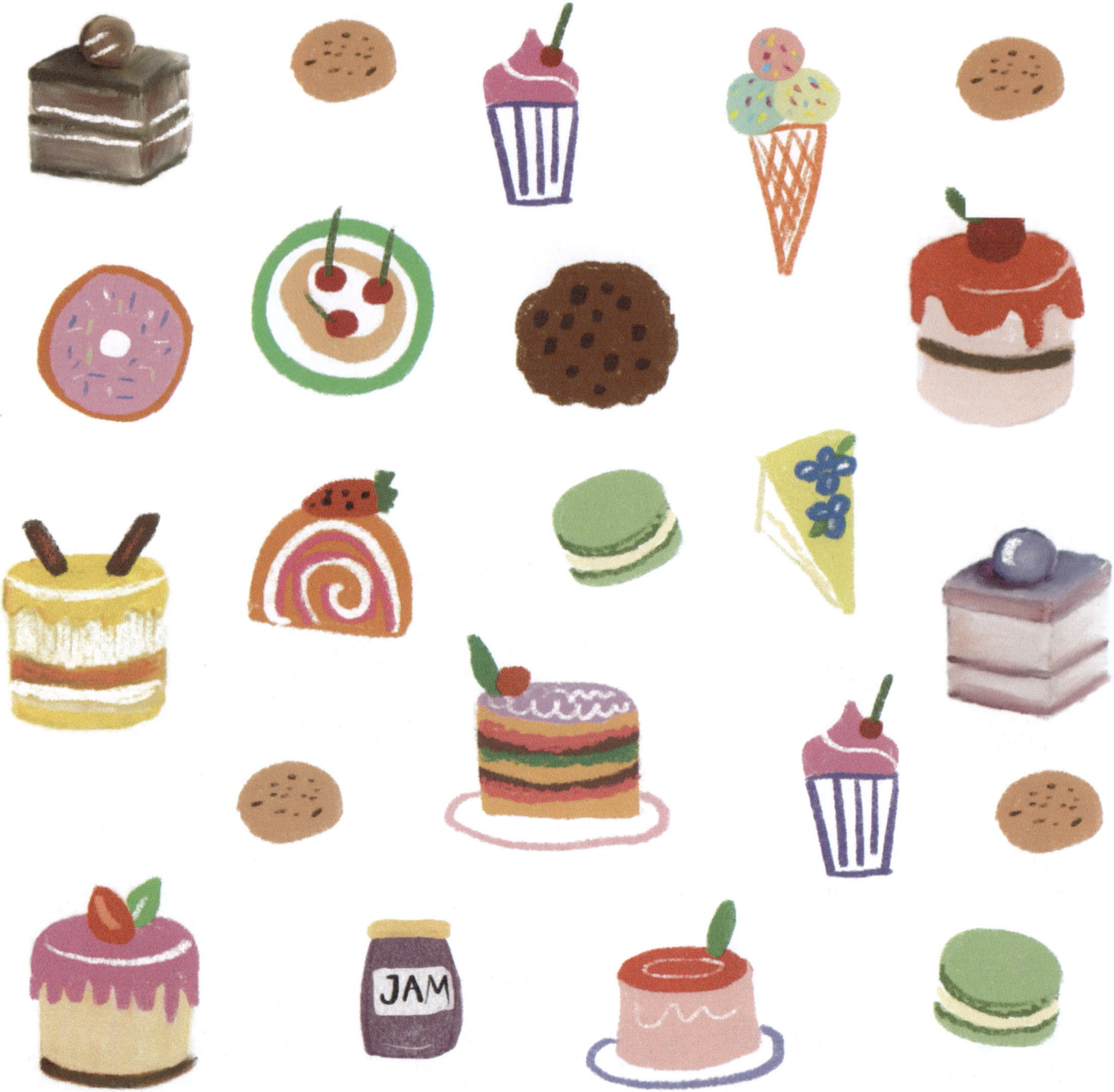
JAM

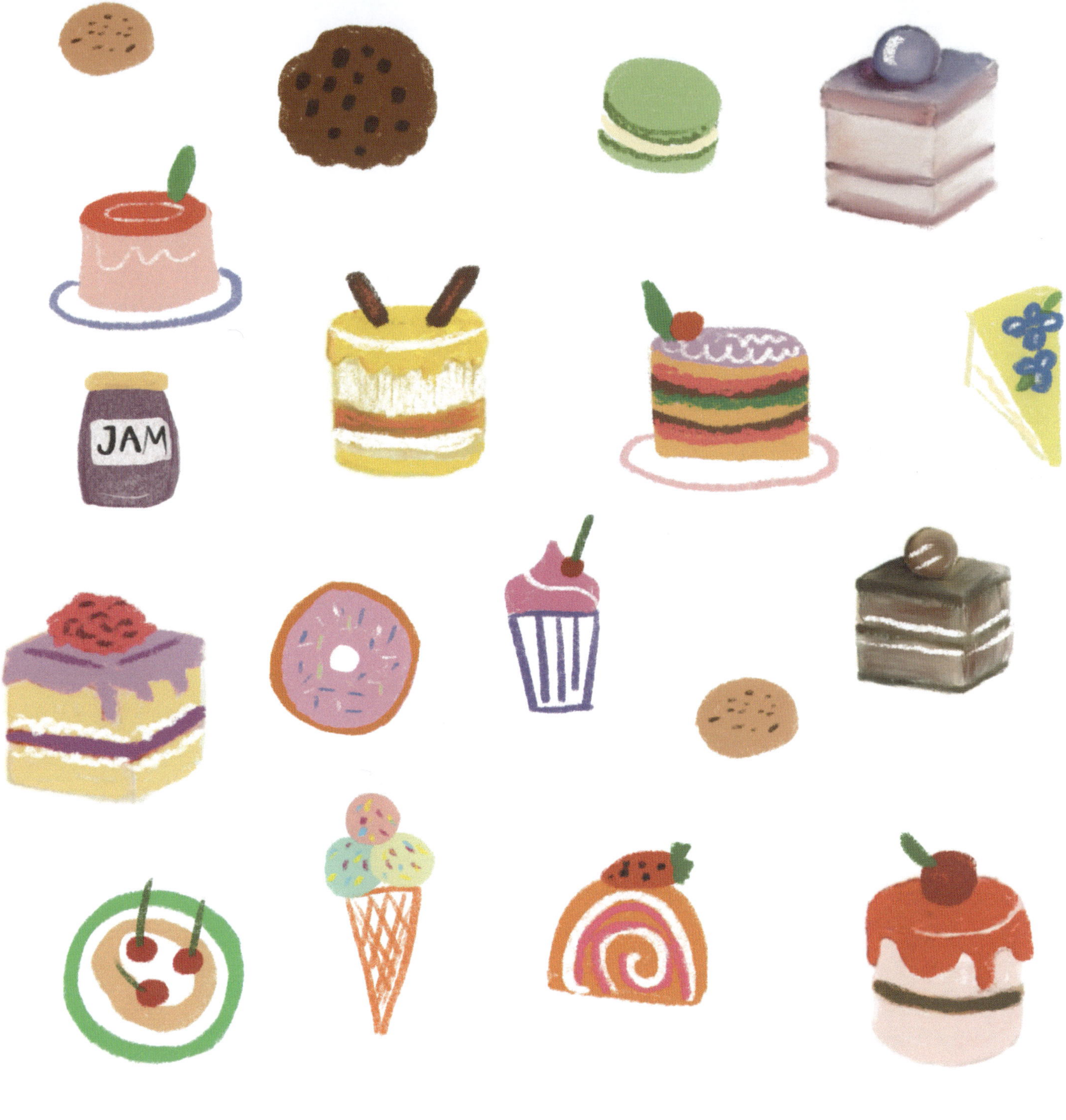
JAM

COPYRIGHT © 2023 MONIKA EVSTATIEVA
All rights reserved.

No part of this book may be reproduced or used in any manner without the prior written permission of the copyright owner, except for the use of brief quotations in a book review and blog article. To request permission send an email at: evstatieva.monika@gmail.com

First edition June 2023
Paperback: ISBN 9798850255534
Printed by Amazon
Written in English

Sweet delights from around the world

by Monika Evstatieva

Welcome to "Sweet Delights from Around the World"! Prepare to embark on a captivating culinary journey that will transport you to distant lands, immerse you in vibrant cultures, and awaken your senses to a symphony of flavors and aromas. This book is an invitation to indulge in the enchanting world of desserts, where each page unveils a treasure trove of sweet delicacies rooted in rich traditions and heritage.

The recipes you will see in this book have been meticulously selected to showcase some of the most beloved and iconic desserts from various corners of the globe. My bigest hope for you is that as you venture into the kitchen you will not only tantalize your taste buds but also ignite your creativity and curiosity. Let the joy of baking fill your heart and bring a sense of fulfillment and satisfaction. It is my sincerest wish that you find joy and have a wonderful time exploring these recipes, discovering new techniques, and making each creation uniquely your own.

In the spirit of culinary adventure, I invite you to embrace the wonderful diversity of the world's desserts and approach your time in the kitchen with a sense of playfulness and fun. Let the aromas wafting from your oven transport you to faraway places, and may each bite be a delightful celebration of cultural richness and global connections.

Whether you are an experienced baker or just beginning your journey into the realm of sweets, this book is meant to be a companion, inspiring and guiding you along the way.

Enjoy the process of bringing these recipes to life, and may the joy of sharing these delectable treats with your loved ones fill your heart with warmth and create lasting memories.

With love,
Monika

save a room have for
little It's little surprise time
moment bite for dessert love

- 11. France
- 13. Singapoor
- 15. Lebanon
- 17. Germany
- 19. Hungary
- 21. Australia
- 23. Iran
- 25. Scotland
- 27. USA
- 29. Switzerland
- 31. Portugal
- 33. Israel

- 37. Colombia
- 15. New Zealand
- 49. Netherlands
- 39. Nicaragua
- 17. Ireland
- 51. Philippines
- 41. Romania
- 35. Cuba
- 43. Czech Republic
- 55. Slovenia
- 53. Croatia

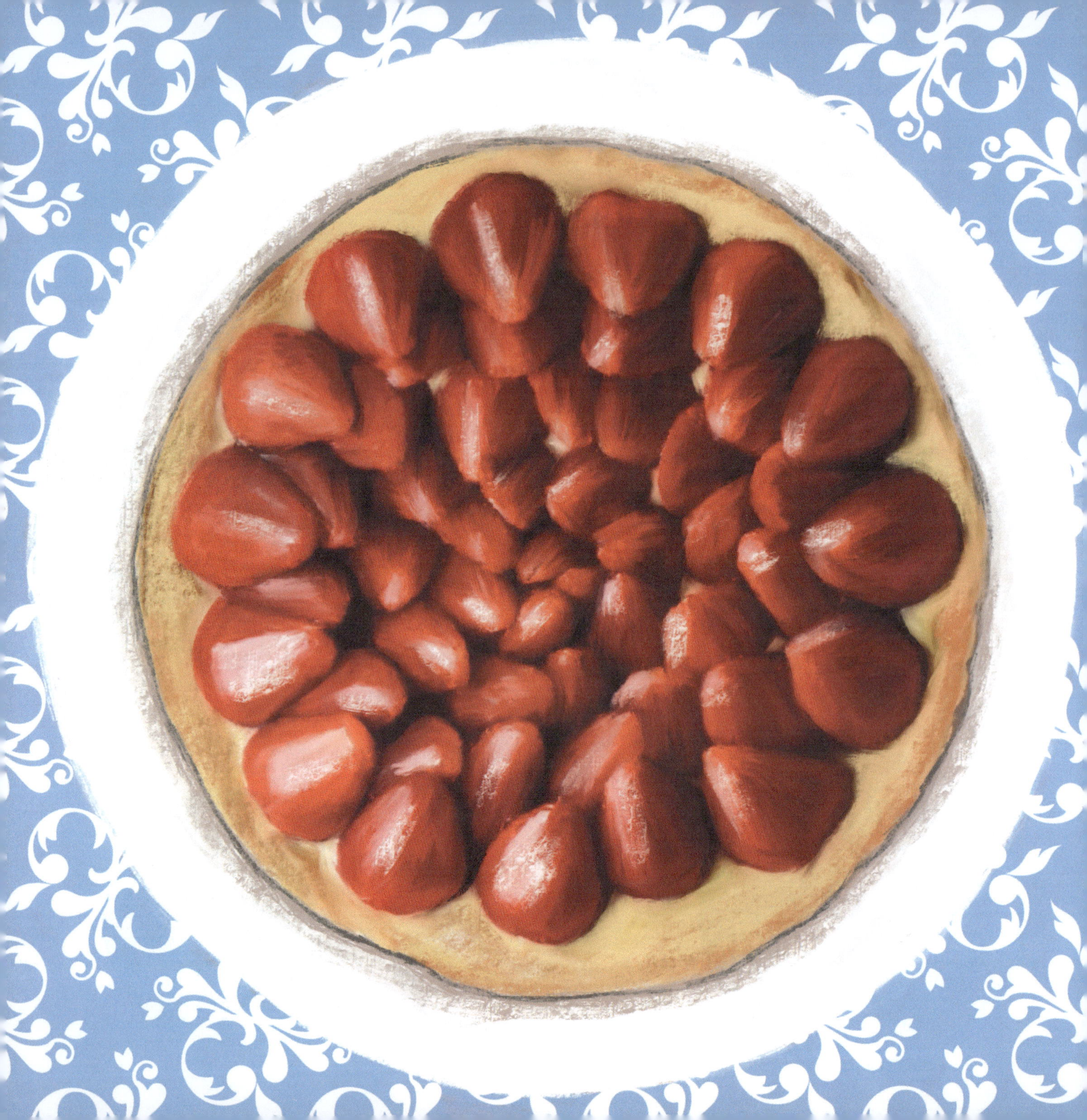

Tarte aux Fraises
(France)

Ingredients:

For the tart shell:
- 1 1/2 cups (190g) all-purpose flour
- 1/4 cup (50g) granulated sugar
- 1/4 teaspoon salt
- 1/2 cup (113g) cold unsalted butter, cubed
- 1 large egg yolk
- 2 tablespoons ice water (or more if needed)

For the filling:
- 1 pound (450g) fresh strawberries, hulled and halved
- 1/2 cup (120ml) heavy cream
- 1/4 cup (50g) granulated sugar
- 1 teaspoon vanilla extract

For the glaze:
- 1/4 cup (60ml) strawberry jam or jelly
- 1 tablespoon water

Instructions:

1. Prepare the tart shell by combining flour, sugar, and salt. Cut in cold butter until the mixture resembles crumbs. Add egg yolk and ice water, mixing until the dough comes together. Chill, then roll out and press into a tart pan. Bake until golden brown.
2. Whip heavy cream, sugar, and vanilla extract until soft peaks form. Spread whipped cream over the cooled tart shell.
3. Arrange halved strawberries on top of the whipped cream.
4. Heat strawberry jam or jelly with water in a saucepan until smooth. Brush the glaze over the strawberries.
5. Refrigerate the tart for 1-2 hours to allow the flavors to meld and the glaze to set.
6. Serve chilled. If desired, you can add a layer of pastry cream or custard as a base, garnish with mint leaves, or dust with powdered sugar.

Indulge in the epitome of French elegance with Tarte aux Fraises, a symphony of buttery tart shell, pillowy whipped cream, and vibrant, sun-kissed strawberries—a timeless masterpiece that celebrates the harmony of flavors and the artistry of French pastry.

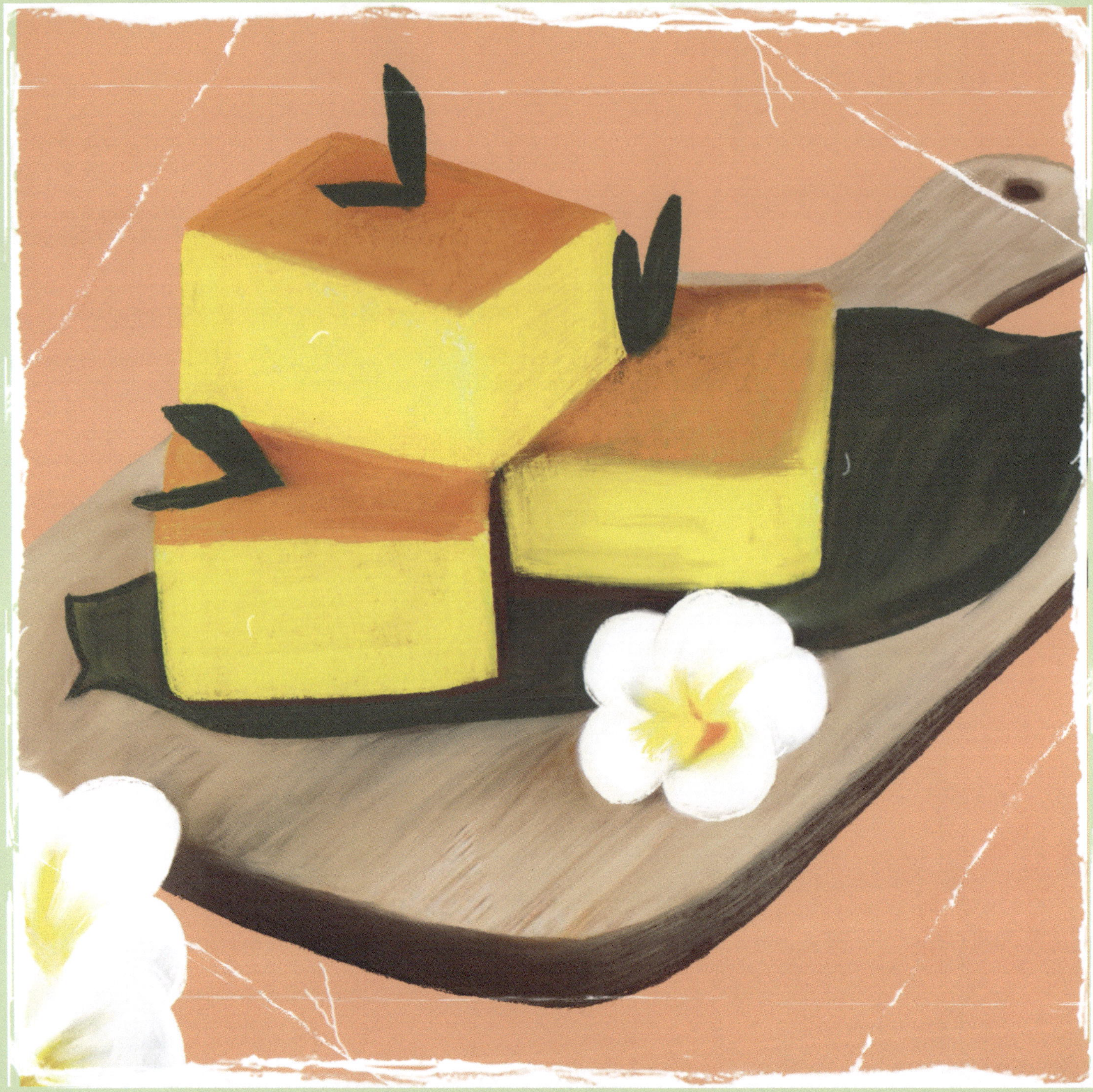

Bingka Ubi

(Singapoore)

Ingredients:

- 500g grated tapioca (cassava)
- 200ml coconut milk
- 150g sugar
- 3 eggs
- 1/2 teaspoon salt
- 4 pandan leaves (optional, for flavor and color)

Instructions:

1. Preheat your oven to 180°C (350°F). Grease a baking dish or individual molds and set them aside.
2. If using pandan leaves, wash them and tie them into knots. Place them in a saucepan with the coconut milk and warm over low heat for a few minutes to infuse the flavor. Remove the pandan leaves and set aside the coconut milk.
3. In a mixing bowl, combine the grated tapioca, sugar, salt, and the infused coconut milk. Mix well until the sugar is dissolved.
4. Beat the eggs in a separate bowl, then add them to the tapioca mixture. Stir until everything is well combined.
5. Pour the batter into the greased baking dish or molds, spreading it evenly.
6. Place the dish or molds in the preheated oven and bake for about 45 minutes to 1 hour, or until the top turns golden brown and the cake is set. You can test for doneness by inserting a toothpick into the center—it should come out clean.
7. Once baked, remove from the oven and allow it to cool in the dish or molds for a few minutes.
8. Serve Bingka Ubi warm or at room temperature, either directly from the baking dish or by cutting it into squares or wedges.

Enjoy this traditional dessert from Singapore with a cup of tea or coffee. Feel free to experiment with additional ingredients such as coconut flakes, pandan extract, or even a sprinkle of grated palm sugar on top for added flavor and visual appeal.

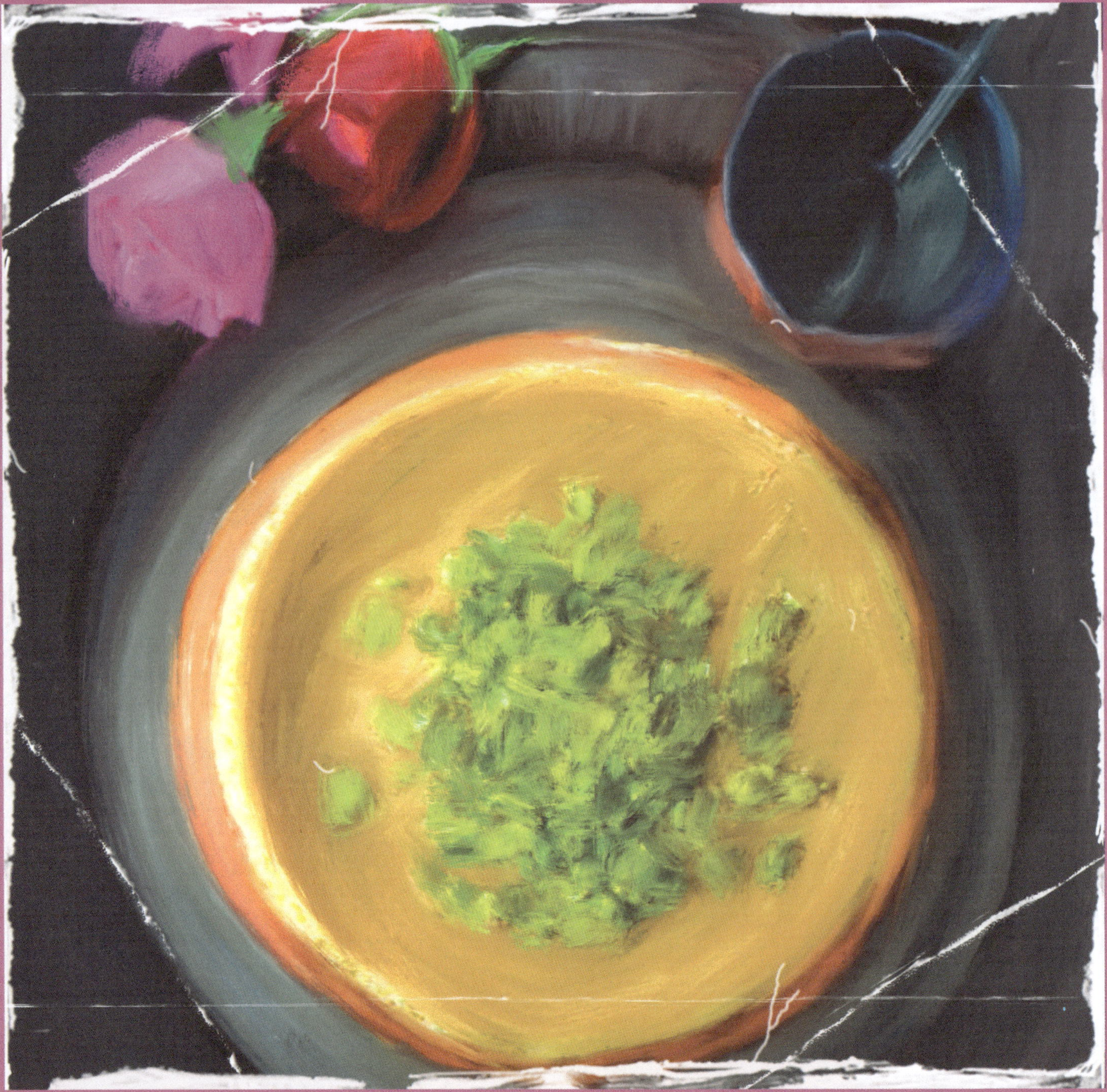

Knafeh
(Lebanon)

Ingredients:

For the Knafeh base:
- 1 pound shredded Knafeh dough (kataifi)
- 1 cup unsalted butter, melted
- 1 tablespoon rosewater (optional)

For the cheese filling:
- 1 pound Akkawi cheese or Mozzarella cheese, shredded
- 1/2 cup fine semolina

For the sugar syrup:
- 1 1/2 cups granulated sugar
- 1 cup water
- 1 tablespoon lemon juice
- 1 tablespoon orange blossom water

For garnish:
- Ground pistachios or slivered almonds

Instructions:

1. Preheat your oven to 350°F (175°C).
2. Start by preparing the sugar syrup. In a saucepan, combine the granulated sugar, water, lemon juice, and orange blossom water. Bring to a boil over medium heat, stirring until the sugar dissolves. Reduce the heat and let it simmer for 10 minutes. Remove from heat and let the syrup cool.
3. In a separate bowl, mix the shredded cheese with the semolina until well combined.
4. Place the shredded knafeh dough in a large bowl and pour the melted butter over it. Mix gently to ensure the dough is evenly coated with butter. Add rosewater if desired and continue to mix.
5. Grease a 9x13-inch baking dish with butter. Spread half of the knafeh dough evenly on the bottom of the dish, pressing it down gently.
6. Spread the cheese mixture over the knafeh dough, ensuring it covers the entire surface evenly.
7. Cover the cheese layer with the remaining knafeh dough, pressing it down gently.
8. Bake in the preheated oven for about 30-35 minutes, or until the knafeh turns golden brown.
9. Once baked, remove the knafeh from the oven and immediately pour the cooled sugar syrup over it, making sure to cover the entire surface.
10. Allow the knafeh to cool slightly before cutting it into squares or diamond-shaped piece.
11. Garnish each piece with ground pistachios or slivered almonds.

Enjoy this sweet delight with family and friends, celebrating the traditions of Lebanese cuisine.

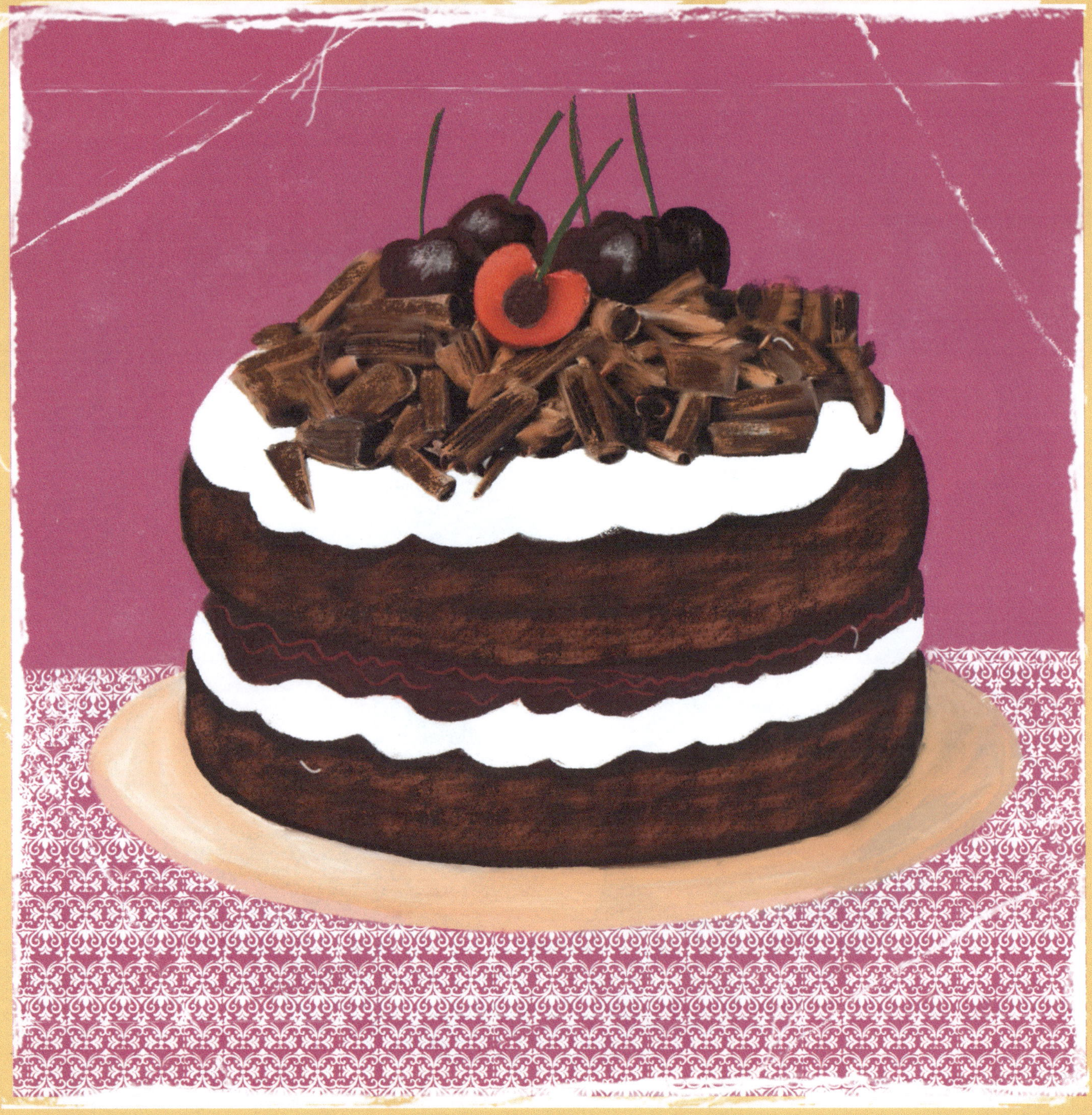

Black forest cake

(Germany)

Ingredients:

For the cake layers:
- 200g (1 ⅔ cups) all-purpose flour
- 50g (½ cup) unsweetened cocoa powder
- 1 ½ teaspoons baking powder
- ¼ teaspoon salt
- 200g (1 cup) granulated sugar
- 4 large eggs
- 120ml (½ cup) milk
- 120ml (½ cup) vegetable oil
- 1 teaspoon vanilla extract

For the cherry filling:
- 600g (4 cups) pitted cherries, fresh or canned
- 100g (½ cup) granulated sugar
- 2 tablespoons cornstarch
- 1 tablespoon lemon juice

For the whipped cream frosting:
- 500ml (2 cups) heavy cream, chilled
- 50g (¼ cup) powdered sugar
- 1 teaspoon vanilla extract

For decoration:
- Dark chocolate shavings
- Additional cherries

Instructions:

1. Preheat your oven to 180°C (350°F). Grease and flour two 9-inch round cake pans.
2. In a medium bowl, whisk together the flour, cocoa powder, baking powder, and salt.
3. In a separate large bowl, beat the sugar and eggs until light and fluffy. Add the milk, vegetable oil, and vanilla extract. Mix until well combined.
4. Gradually add the dry ingredients to the wet ingredients, mixing until the batter is smooth.
5. Divide the batter evenly between the prepared cake pans. Smooth the tops with a spatula.
6. Bake in the preheated oven for about 25-30 minutes or until a toothpick inserted into the center comes out clean.
7. Remove the cakes from the oven and let them cool in the pans for 10 minutes. Then transfer them to a wire rack to cool completely.
8. Meanwhile, prepare the cherry filling. In a saucepan, combine the cherries, sugar, cornstarch, and lemon juice. Cook over medium heat until the mixture thickens, stirring constantly. Remove from heat and let it cool completely.
9. For the whipped cream frosting, in a chilled bowl, whip the heavy cream, powdered sugar, and vanilla extract until stiff peaks form.
10. Once the cakes are completely cooled, slice each cake horizontally into two equal layers, creating a total of four layers.
11. Place one cake layer on a serving plate. Spread a layer of whipped cream frosting on top. Add a layer of cherry filling. Repeat this process with the remaining cake layers, ending with a layer of whipped cream frosting on top.
12. Use the remaining whipped cream frosting to frost the sides of the cake.
13. Decorate the top of the cake with dark chocolate shavings and additional cherries.
14. Refrigerate the cake for a few hours before serving to allow the flavors to meld.

Enjoy the rich flavors of chocolate, cherries, and whipped cream in this classic German dessert!

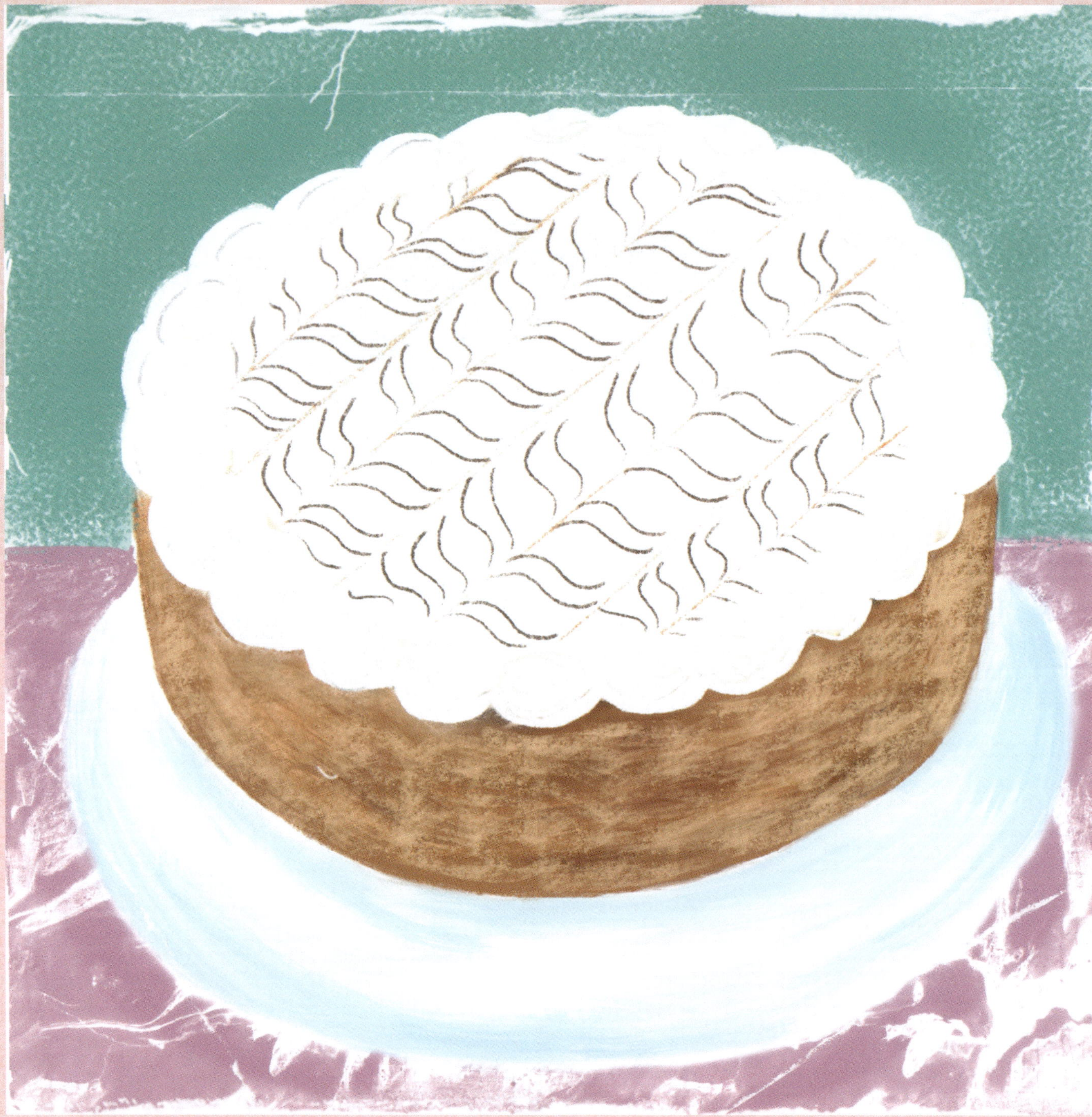

Esterházy torte
(Hungary)

Ingredients:

For the cake layers:
- 6 large eggs, separated
- 200g (1 cup) granulated sugar
- 200g (1 ⅔ cups) ground walnuts
- 2 tablespoons all-purpose flour
- 1 teaspoon vanilla extract

For the buttercream filling:
- 250g (1 ¼ cups) unsalted butter, softened
- 250g (2 ½ cups) powdered sugar
- 2 teaspoons vanilla extract
- 2 tablespoons dark cocoa powder
- 2 tablespoons strong brewed coffee

For the glaze:
- 200g (1 ¼ cups) powdered sugar
- 2 tablespoons unsweetened cocoa powder
- 2-3 tablespoons hot water

For decoration:
- Whole walnuts
- Chocolate ganache
- Silver dragées (small silver sugar balls)

Instructions:

1. Follow the instructions for making the cake layers and buttercream filling from the previous recipe.
2. Once the cake layers are assembled with the buttercream filling, prepare the glaze by sifting the powdered sugar and cocoa powder into a bowl. Gradually add hot water, one tablespoon at a time, until a smooth, pourable consistency is achieved. Mix well to remove any lumps.
3. Pour the glaze over the top of the cake, allowing it to drizzle down the sides. Use a spatula or the back of a spoon to help spread the glaze evenly.
4. After spreading the glaze, create a traditional decoration on top of the cake. Start by piping lines of chocolate ganache across the cake in a lattice pattern. You can use a piping bag fitted with a small round tip to achieve this.
5. Place whole walnuts at the intersection points of the chocolate ganache lattice.
6. Finally, place silver dragées on the outer edges of the cake, following the pattern of the lattice.
7. Refrigerate the cake for a few hours to allow the flavors to meld and the glaze to set.

Slice and serve the beautifully decorated Eszterházy torta, and enjoy the delicious layers of cake, buttercream, and chocolate ganache.

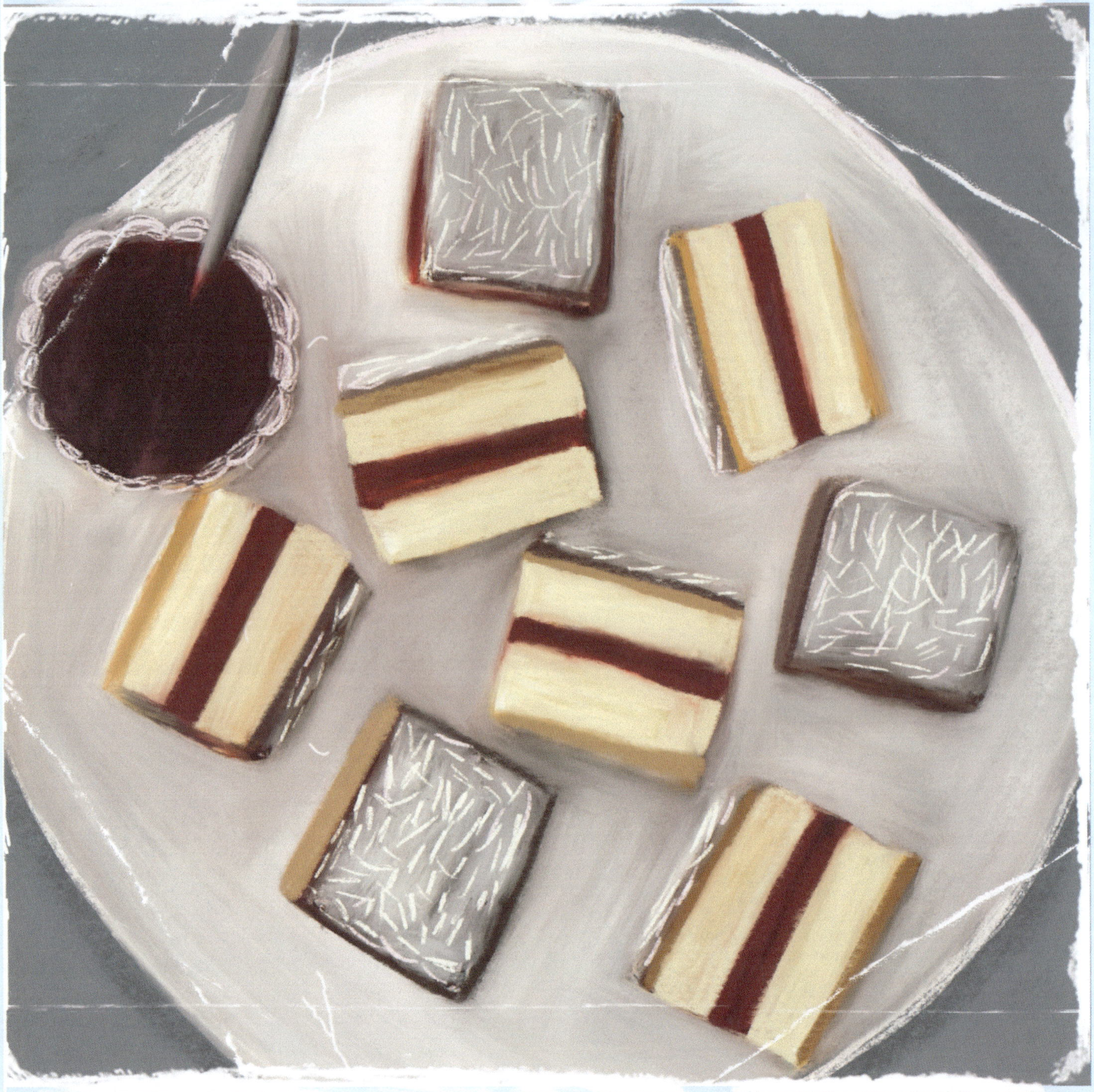

Lamingtons

(Australia)

Ingredients:

- 2 1/2 cups all-purpose flour
- 1 1/2 teaspoons baking powder
- 1/2 teaspoon salt
- 1/2 cup unsalted butter, softened
- 1 cup granulated sugar
- 3 large eggs
- 1 teaspoon vanilla extract
- 1 cup milk
- 4 cups desiccated coconut
- 2 cups powdered sugar
- 1/4 cup unsweetened cocoa powder
- 1/2 cup boiling water
- 4 tablespoons unsalted butter, melted

Instructions:

1. Preheat your oven to 350°F (175°C). Grease and line a 9x13-inch baking pan with parchment paper.
2. In a mixing bowl, sift together the flour, baking powder, and salt. Set aside.
3. In a separate large bowl, cream together the softened butter and granulated sugar until light and fluffy.
4. Add the eggs one at a time, beating well after each addition. Stir in the vanilla extract.
5. Gradually add the flour mixture to the butter mixture, alternating with the milk, beginning and ending with the flour mixture. Mix until just combined.
6. Pour the batter into the prepared baking pan, spreading it out evenly.
7. Bake in the preheated oven for about 25-30 minutes, or until a toothpick inserted into the center comes out clean.
8. Remove the cake from the oven and let it cool completely in the pan.
9. Once the cake is cooled, cut it into squares or rectangles of desired size.
10. Place the desiccated coconut in a shallow bowl.
11. In a separate bowl, sift together the powdered sugar and cocoa powder. Add the boiling water and melted butter, and stir until smooth and well combined.
12. Using two forks or a fork and a spoon, dip each cake square into the chocolate mixture, allowing any excess to drip off.
13. Immediately roll the chocolate-coated cake square in the desiccated coconut, ensuring all sides are coated.
14. Place the coated Lamingtons on a wire rack to set.
15. Repeat the dipping and coating process with the remaining cake squares.
16. Allow the Lamingtons to set at room temperature for a few hours before serving.

Enjoy these delightful Australian Lamingtons, with their tender cake interior, rich chocolate coating, and coconut crunch. They are a true Aussie classic, perfect for afternoon tea or any special occasion

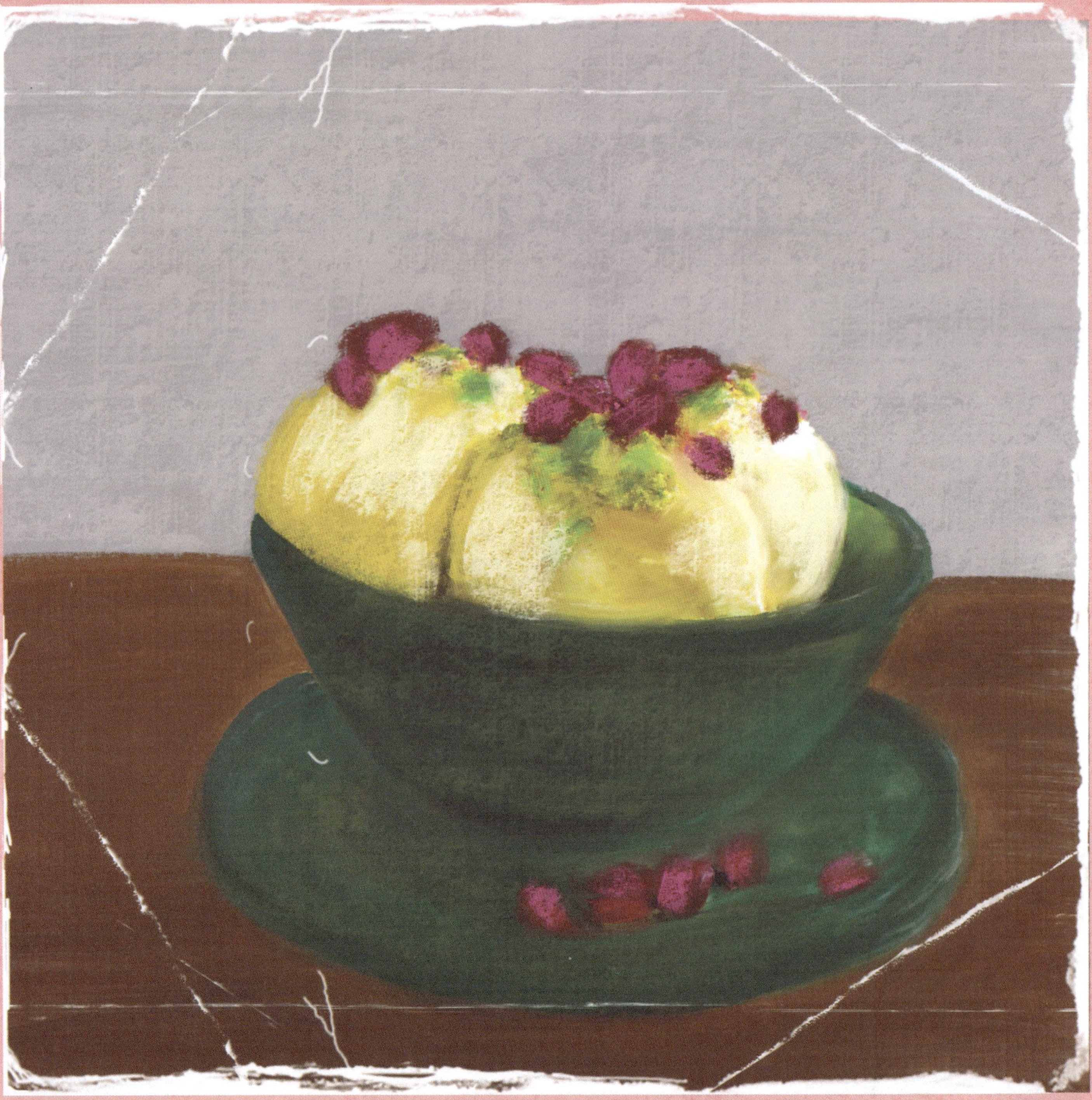

Bastani Sonnati
(Iran)

Ingredients:

- 2 cups heavy cream
- 1 cup whole milk
- 3/4 cup granulated sugar
- 4 large egg yolks
- 1 teaspoon pure vanilla extract
- 1/2 teaspoon ground saffron threads
- 1/4 cup rosewater
- 1/2 cup chopped pistachios (optional)

Instructions:

1. In a saucepan, combine the heavy cream and milk. Heat over medium heat until it starts to simmer. Remove from heat.
2. In a separate bowl, whisk together the sugar and egg yolks until well combined.
3. Slowly pour a small amount of the hot cream mixture into the egg mixture, whisking constantly to prevent the eggs from scrambling. Gradually add more of the hot cream mixture while whisking continuously.
4. Pour the mixture back into the saucepan and place it over medium-low heat. Cook, stirring constantly, until the mixture thickens and coats the back of a spoon. This usually takes about 5-7 minutes. Do not let it boil.
5. Remove the saucepan from heat and stir in the vanilla extract and ground saffron threads. Mix well to incorporate the saffron flavor.
6. Pour the mixture into a bowl and let it cool to room temperature. Then cover the bowl and refrigerate for at least 4 hours or overnight to chill completely.
7. Once the mixture is chilled, stir in the rosewater. If desired, add the chopped pistachios to the mixture and mix well.
8. Pour the mixture into an ice cream maker and churn according to the manufacturer's instructions until it reaches a soft, creamy consistency.
9. Transfer the ice cream to a lidded container and freeze for an additional 4 hours or until firm.
10. Serve the saffron ice cream in bowls or cones, and garnish with additional pistachios if desired.

Enjoy the delightful flavors of homemade saffron ice cream, a delicious treat from Iran!

Hunte
AUGUST SCA
PER & SONS
REAM
ALWAYS READY FOR USE.
Reliabl
MUSICAL INSTRUMENTS.
FARMER CHAR
We design the handles
for durable and reliable
service. Each hand
LARK
PIANOS
Clearance
Sale.
JOHN CAMPB
COOL
SWEET SCENTS
Complimentary Presents
GIFTS
Guaranteed to Retai
Splendid Appearance,
Wear like Silver for
years.
FINE CLOTHING
THE QUEEN, THE EMPRESS FREDERICK,
Public with Every Description of
MENS CLOTHING

Empire biscuits
(Scotland)

Ingredients:

For the biscuits:
- 1 cup unsalted butter, softened
- 1/2 cup granulated sugar
- 2 cups all-purpose flour
- 1/4 cup cornstarch (cornflour)

For the filling and decoration:
- Raspberry jam (or your preferred jam)
- 1 cup powdered sugar (icing sugar)
- 2-3 tablespoons water
- Glace cherries

Instructions:

1. Preheat your oven to 350°F (180°C) and line two baking sheets with parchment paper.
2. In a mixing bowl, cream together the softened butter and granulated sugar until light and fluffy.
3. Sift in the flour and cornstarch and mix until the ingredients come together to form a dough.
4. Roll out the dough on a floured surface to a thickness of about 1/4 inch (0.6 cm). Use a round cookie cutter to cut out biscuit rounds. Place them on the prepared baking sheets.
5. Bake in the preheated oven for approximately 12-15 minutes or until the biscuits are just starting to turn golden around the edges.
6. Remove from the oven and transfer the biscuits to a wire rack to cool completely.
7. Once the biscuits have cooled, spread a layer of raspberry jam on the underside of one biscuit. Place another biscuit on top to create a sandwich.
8. In a small bowl, mix the powdered sugar with enough water to make a smooth and thick icing consistency.
9. Spoon a small amount of icing onto the center of each biscuit and place a glace cherry on top.
10. Allow the icing to set before serving.

Let each bite transport you to the picturesque landscapes of Scotland, where time-honored recipes are cherished and shared with loved ones.

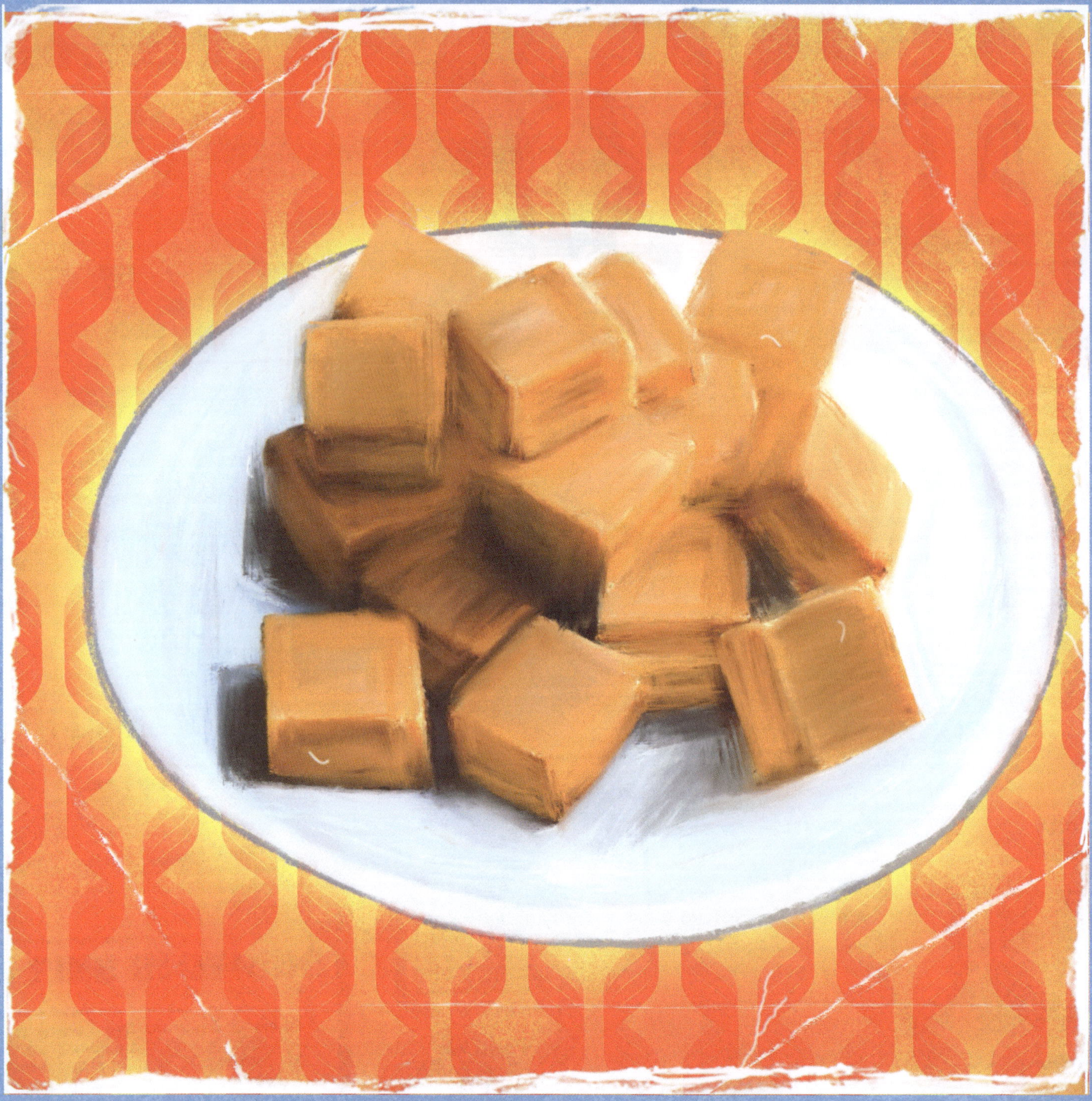

Fudge
(USA)

Ingredients:

- 2 cups granulated sugar
- 1 cup heavy cream
- 1/4 cup unsalted butter
- 1 teaspoon vanilla extract
- 1 1/2 cups semisweet chocolate chips
- 1 cup chopped nuts (such as walnuts or pecans), optional

Instructions:

1. Grease an 8x8-inch baking dish or line it with parchment paper.
2. In a medium-sized saucepan, combine the sugar, heavy cream, and butter. Place the saucepan over medium heat and stir until the sugar dissolves and the mixture comes to a boil.
3. Once boiling, continue cooking the mixture without stirring until it reaches the soft-ball stage on a candy thermometer (around 235°F or 115°C). If you don't have a thermometer, you can perform the soft-ball test by dropping a small amount of the mixture into a glass of cold water. It should form a soft ball that can be flattened with your fingers.
4. Remove the saucepan from the heat and let it cool for about 5 minutes.
5. Add the vanilla extract, chocolate chips, and nuts (if using) to the saucepan. Stir the mixture vigorously until the chocolate chips are completely melted and the mixture is smooth and glossy.
6. Pour the fudge mixture into the prepared baking dish, spreading it evenly.
7. Let the fudge cool at room temperature until it reaches room temperature. You can also place it in the refrigerator to speed up the cooling process.
8. Once cooled and set, cut the fudge into small squares or rectangles.
9. Store the fudge in an airtight container at room temperature or in the refrigerator.

Treat yourself to a moment of pure bliss with every bite of this beloved American confection.

Carac 🇨🇭

(Switzerland)

Ingredients:

- 2 cups all-purpose flour
- 1/2 cup unsalted butter, softened
- 1/2 cup granulated sugar
- 1 egg
- 1 teaspoon vanilla extract
- 1/4 teaspoon salt
- 1/2 cup apricot jam (or jam of your choice)
- Powdered sugar, for dusting

Instructions:

1. Preheat your oven to 350°F (175°C) and line a baking sheet with parchment paper.
2. In a mixing bowl, cream together the softened butter and granulated sugar until light and fluffy.
3. Add the egg and vanilla extract to the butter-sugar mixture and beat until well combined.
4. In a separate bowl, whisk together the all-purpose flour and salt. Gradually add the flour mixture to the wet ingredients, mixing until the dough comes together.
5. Turn the dough out onto a lightly floured surface and knead it briefly to ensure it is well combined. Divide the dough into two equal portions.
6. Roll out one portion of the dough to a thickness of about 1/8 inch (3 mm). Use a round cookie cutter to cut out circles from the dough.
7. Transfer the circles to the prepared baking sheet, spacing them about 1 inch (2.5 cm) apart. Repeat the process with the second portion of dough.
8. Using your thumb or the back of a spoon, create a small indentation in the center of each cookie.
9. Fill each indentation with a small dollop of apricot jam or your preferred jam flavor.
10. Bake the cookies in the preheated oven for about 12-15 minutes, or until the edges turn golden brown.
11. Remove the cookies from the oven and allow them to cool on the baking sheet for a few minutes. Then transfer them to a wire rack to cool completely.
12. Once the cookies are cooled, dust them with powdered sugar.

Let the magic of Swiss Carac transport you to the breathtaking beauty of Switzerland, where every indulgent moment is a celebration of exquisite taste and captivating culture.

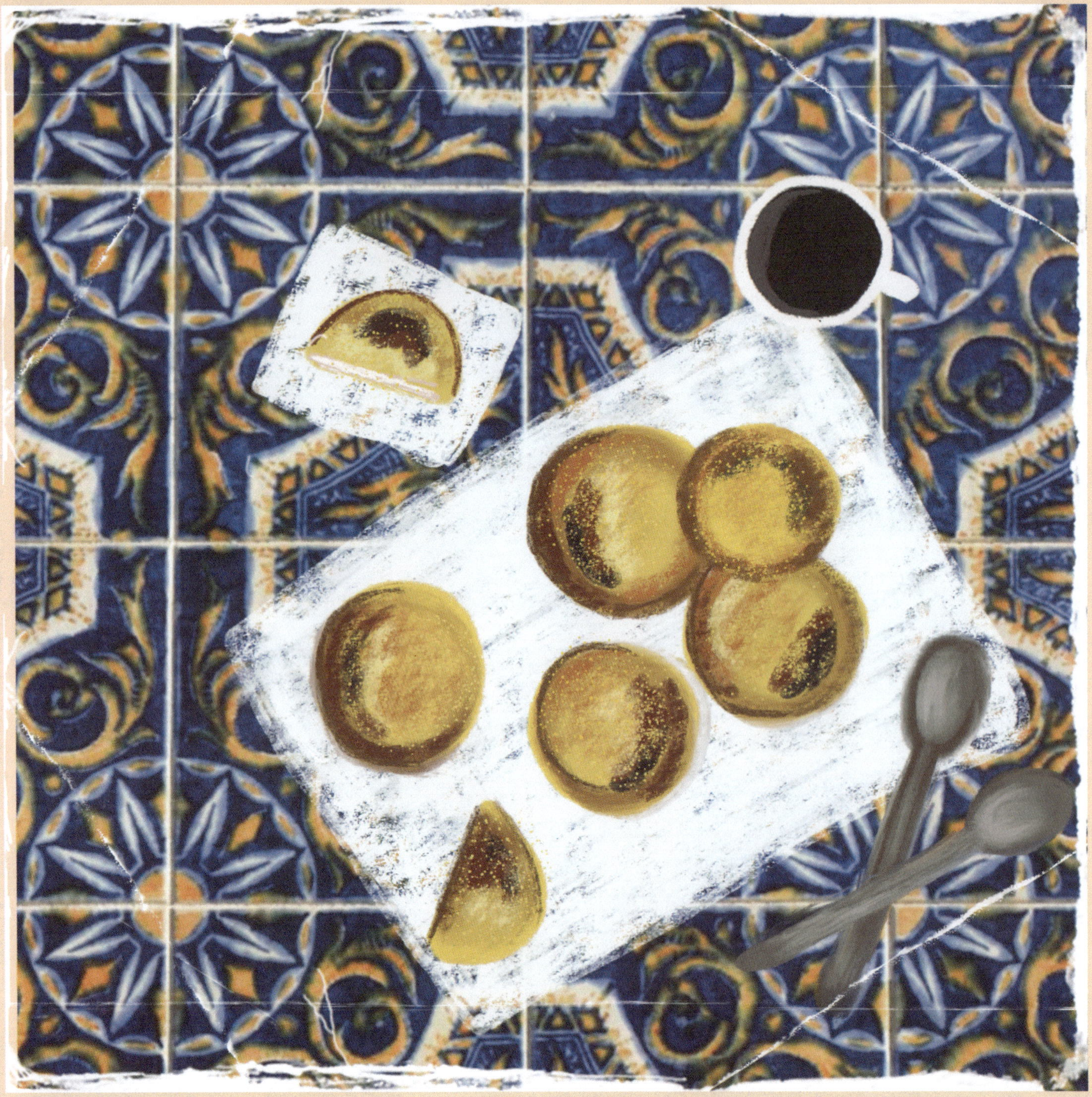

Pastel de nata

(Portugal)

Ingredients:

For the pastry:
- 2 sheets of pre-made puff pastry (or you can make your own)
- Butter or cooking spray, for greasing

For the custard filling:
- 2 cups whole milk
- 1 cinnamon stick
- 1 strip of lemon peel (about 2 inches long)
- 1 cup granulated sugar
- 1/4 cup all-purpose flour
- 6 large egg yolks
- 1 teaspoon vanilla extract

For the topping:
- Powdered sugar (optional)
- Ground cinnamon (optional)

Instructions:

1. Preheat your oven to 475°F (245°C).
2. Grease a muffin tin or tart pans with butter or cooking spray.
3. Roll out the puff pastry sheets on a floured surface to a thickness of about 1/8 inch (3 mm). Cut out circles slightly larger than the size of the muffin cups or tart pans.
4. Line each greased cup or pan with the puff pastry circles, pressing them gently into the bottom and sides. Trim any excess dough if necessary.
5. In a saucepan, heat the milk, cinnamon stick, and lemon peel over medium heat until it starts to simmer. Remove from heat and let it infuse for about 10 minutes. Then strain out the cinnamon stick and lemon peel.
6. In a mixing bowl, whisk together the sugar and flour. Gradually whisk in the egg yolks until smooth and well combined.
7. Slowly pour the warm milk into the egg mixture, whisking continuously to prevent curdling.
8. Transfer the mixture back to the saucepan and cook over medium heat, stirring constantly, until it thickens and coats the back of a spoon. This usually takes about 5-7 minutes. Stir in the vanilla extract.
9. Remove the custard from the heat and let it cool slightly.
10. Spoon the custard into the prepared puff pastry cups, filling them about 3/4 full.
11. Place the muffin tin or tart pans in the preheated oven and bake for about 12-15 minutes or until the pastry is golden brown and the custard is set with a slight wobble in the center.
12. Remove the Pastel de Nata from the oven and let them cool in the tin or pans for a few minutes. Then transfer them to a wire rack to cool completely.
13. Optionally, sprinkle some powdered sugar and ground cinnamon on top of the cooled Pastel de Nata before serving.

Let each bite of this delectable custard tart, make you experience the athmosphere of Portuguese streets where the aroma of freshly baked pastries fills the air. !

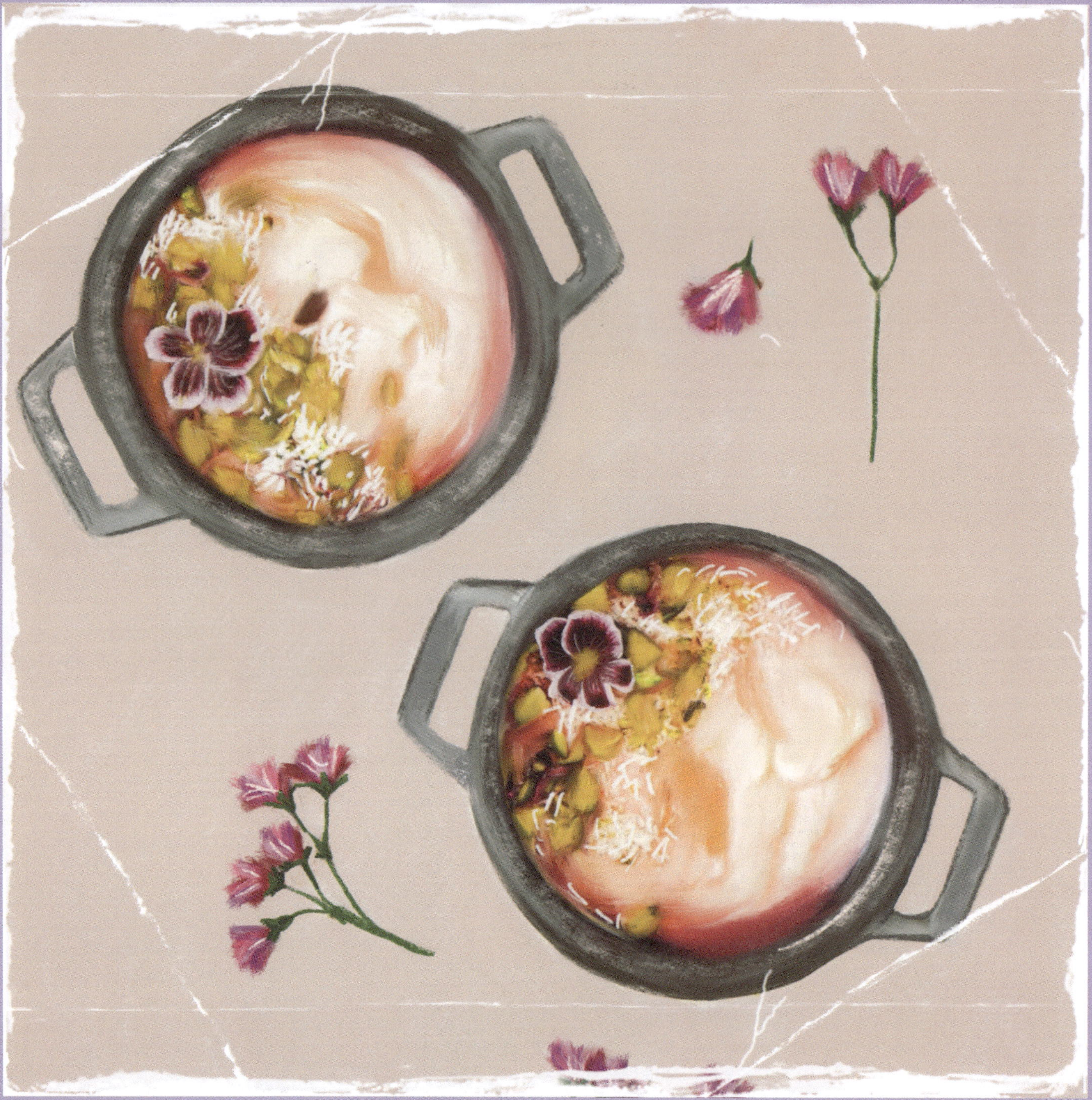

Malabi
(Israel)

Ingredients:

- 4 cups whole milk
- 1/2 cup cornstarch
- 1/2 cup granulated sugar
- 1 tablespoon rosewater
- Optional toppings: crushed pistachios, shredded coconut, or syrup (such as pomegranate or rose syrup)

Instructions:

1. In a medium-sized saucepan, whisk together the milk, cornstarch, and sugar until well combined and no lumps remain.
2. Place the saucepan over medium heat and bring the mixture to a gentle boil, stirring constantly to prevent scorching.
3. Once the mixture thickens and reaches a pudding-like consistency, remove it from the heat.
4. Stir in the rosewater, ensuring it is evenly distributed throughout the mixture.
5. Pour the Malabi into individual serving bowls or a large serving dish. Allow it to cool at room temperature for a few minutes.
6. Once cooled, cover the Malabi and refrigerate for at least 2 hours, or until it is fully set.
7. Before serving, garnish the Malabi with your desired toppings, such as crushed pistachios, shredded coconut, or a drizzle of syrup.
8. Enjoy the Hebrew Malabi chilled, savoring its creamy texture and delicate flavors.

Let the Malabi be your passport to an enchanting world of flavors, where the fusion of ancient and modern influences creates a truly extraordinary dessert experience.

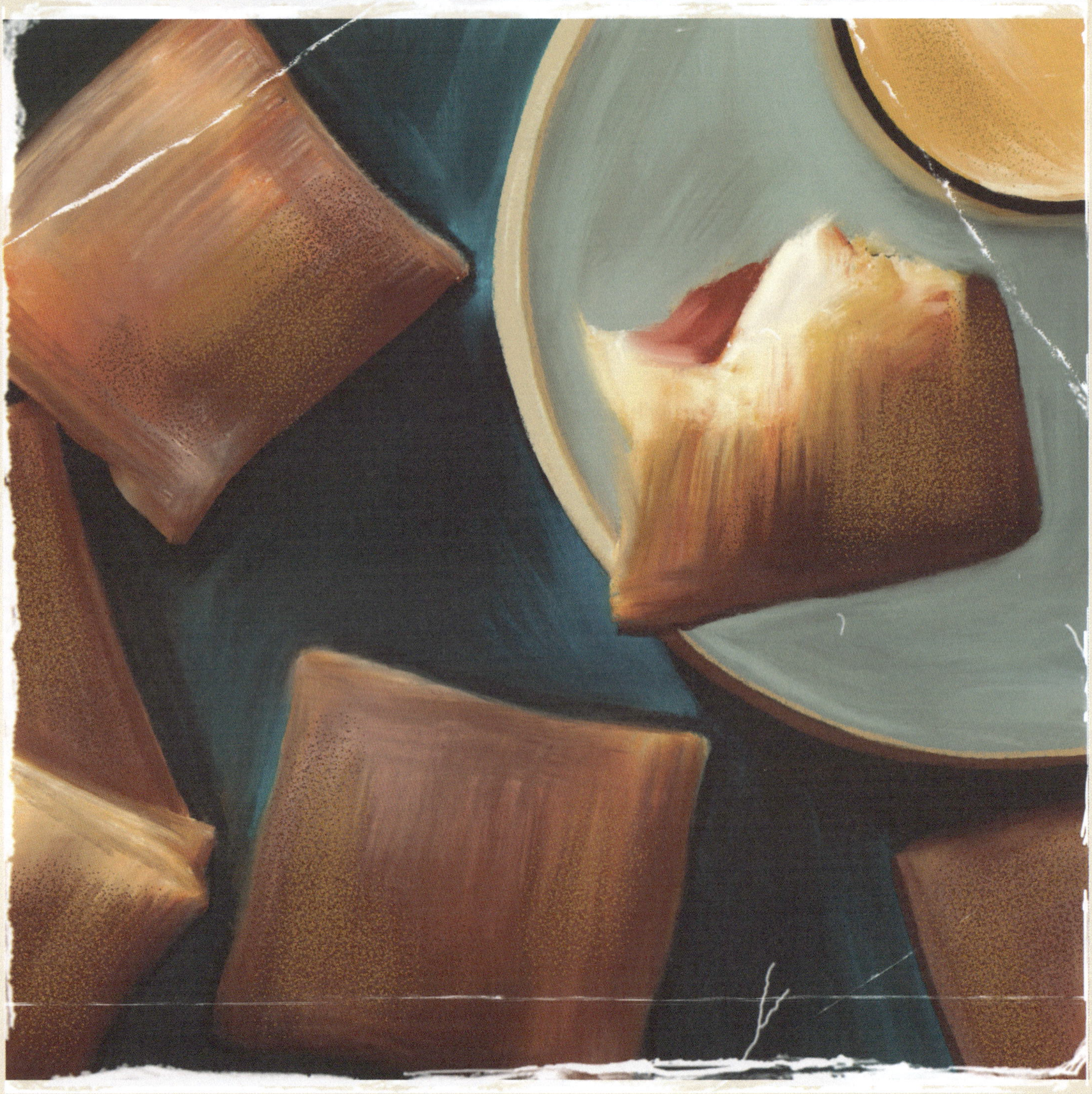

Pastelitos de Guayaba
(Cuba)

Ingredients:

- 1 package of puff pastry sheets (thawed)
- 1 cup guava paste
- 1 egg (beaten, for egg wash)
- Powdered sugar (for dusting)

Instructions:

1. Preheat your oven to 375°F (190°C) and line a baking sheet with parchment paper.
2. Roll out the puff pastry sheets on a lightly floured surface to about 1/8 inch thickness.
3. Cut the puff pastry into squares or rectangles, approximately 4 to 5 inches in size.
4. Cut the guava paste into thin slices or small cubes.
5. Place a slice or cube of guava paste in the center of each pastry square.
6. Fold one corner of the pastry over the guava paste to create a triangle shape. Press the edges firmly to seal.
7. Use a fork to crimp and seal the edges of the pastry triangle.
8. Place the pastelitos on the prepared baking sheet and brush the tops with beaten egg wash.
9. Bake in the preheated oven for about 15-20 minutes, or until the pastelitos turn golden brown and puffy.
10. Remove from the oven and allow the pastelitos to cool on a wire rack.
11. Once cooled, dust the pastelitos with powdered sugar for an extra touch of sweetness.

Serve the Pastelitos de Guayaba as a delightful snack or dessert, and enjoy the combination of flaky pastry and the luscious guava filling.

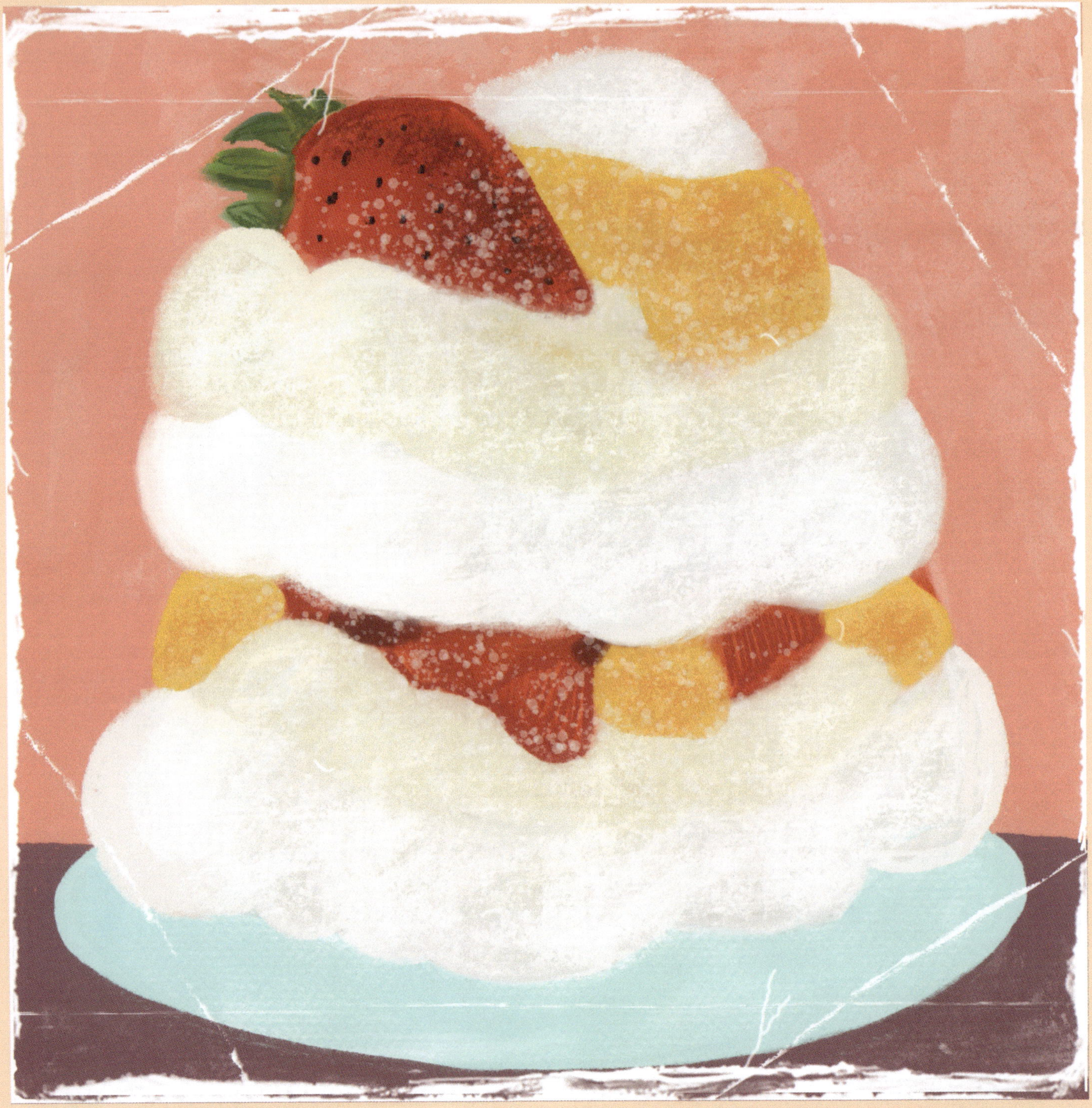

Merengón

(Colombia)

Ingredients:

- Ingredients:
- 4 large egg whites
- 1 cup granulated sugar
- 1 teaspoon vanilla extract
- 1 teaspoon white vinegar
- 1 cup heavy cream
- 2 cups mixed fresh fruits (such as strawberries, bananas, mangoes, or berries)
- 1 tablespoon powdered sugar (optional, for dusting)

Instructions:

- Preheat your oven to 250°F (120°C). Line a baking sheet with parchment paper.
- In a clean, dry mixing bowl, beat the egg whites on medium speed until soft peaks form.
- Gradually add the granulated sugar, a tablespoon at a time, while continuing to beat on high speed. Beat until the mixture is glossy and stiff peaks form.
- Gently fold in the vanilla extract and white vinegar until well incorporated.
- Spoon the meringue mixture onto the prepared baking sheet, shaping it into a large nest or circle, creating a well in the center.
- Bake the meringue in the preheated oven for about 1 hour and 30 minutes, or until the outside is crisp and dry.
- Once baked, remove the meringue from the oven and let it cool completely on the baking sheet.
- In a separate mixing bowl, whip the heavy cream until stiff peaks form.
- Fill the center of the cooled meringue nest with the whipped cream.
- Arrange the fresh fruits on top of the cream, creating a colorful and vibrant display.
- Optional: Dust the top of the fruits with powdered sugar for an extra touch of sweetness.
- Serve the Merengón by slicing into portions, making sure each serving includes a portion of the meringue, whipped cream, and fresh fruits.

Enjoy this delightful Colombian dessert that showcases the sweet and tropical essence of Colombian cuisine.

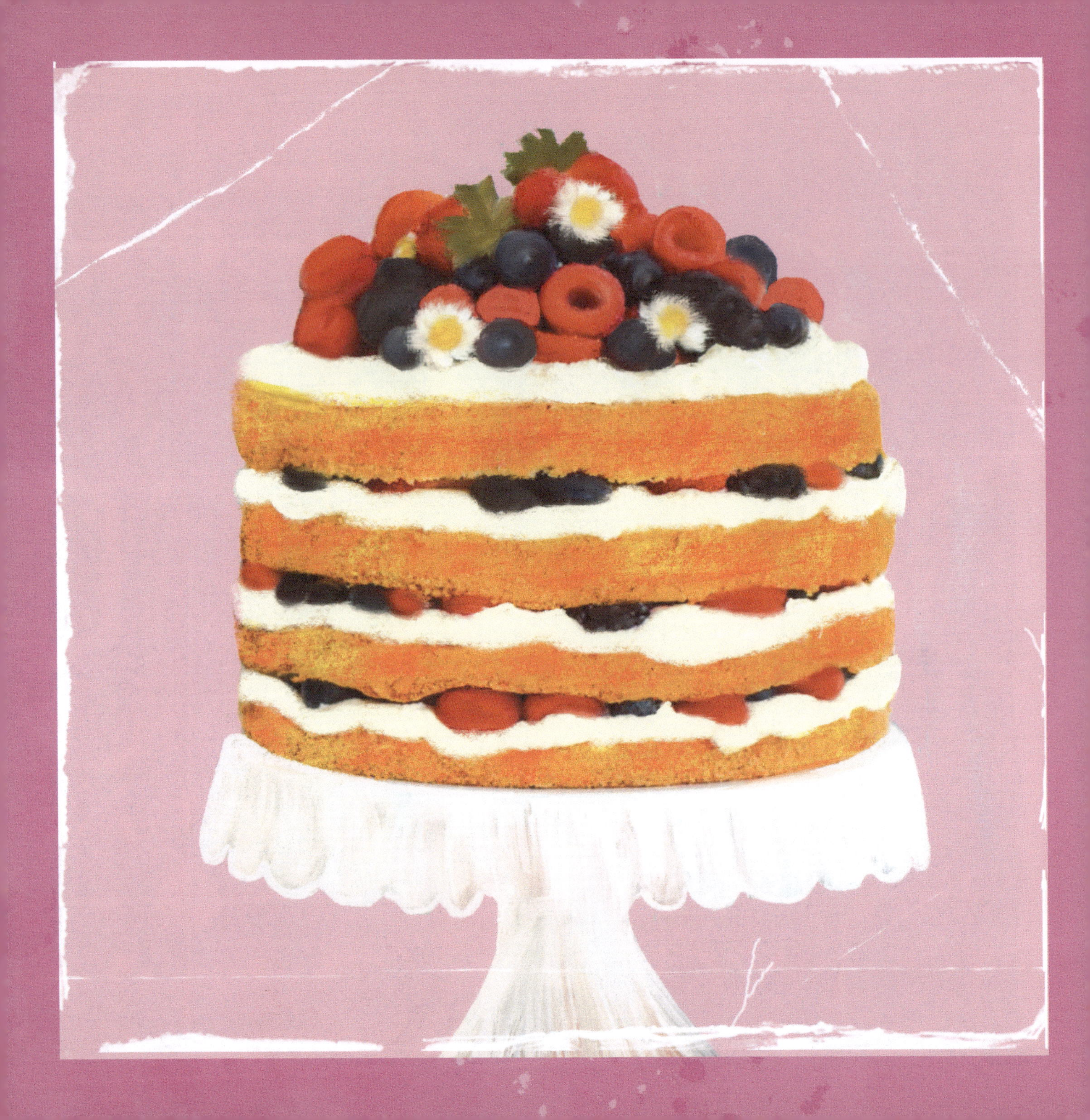

Tres Leches Cake
(Nicaragua)

Ingredients:

For the cake:
- 1 1/2 cups all-purpose flour
- 1 teaspoon baking powder
- 1/2 teaspoon salt
- 1/2 cup unsalted butter, softened
- 1 cup granulated sugar
- 5 large eggs
- 1 teaspoon vanilla extract

For the tres leches mixture:
- 1 can (14 ounces) sweetened condensed milk
- 1 can (12 ounces) evaporated milk
- 1 cup whole milk
- 1 teaspoon vanilla extract

For the whipped cream topping:
- 1 1/2 cups heavy cream
- 3 tablespoons granulated sugar
- 1/2 teaspoon vanilla extract

Instructions:

1. Preheat your oven to 350°F (175°C). Grease and flour a 9x13-inch baking pan.
2. In a medium bowl, whisk together the flour, baking powder, and salt. Set aside.
3. In a large mixing bowl, cream the softened butter and granulated sugar together until light and fluffy.
4. Add the eggs, one at a time, beating well after each addition. Stir in the vanilla extract.
5. Gradually add the flour mixture to the butter mixture, mixing until just combined. Be careful not to overmix.
6. Pour the cake batter into the prepared baking pan and spread it evenly.
7. Bake for about 25-30 minutes, or until a toothpick inserted into the center comes out clean.
8. While the cake is baking, prepare the tres leches mixture. In a mixing bowl, whisk together the sweetened condensed milk, evaporated milk, whole milk, and vanilla extract until well combined. Set aside.
9. Once the cake is baked, remove it from the oven and let it cool in the pan for about 10 minutes.
10. Using a fork or skewer, poke holes all over the surface of the cake.
11. Slowly pour the tres leches mixture over the warm cake, allowing it to seep into the holes. Let the cake cool completely and absorb the liquid.
12. In the meantime, prepare the whipped cream topping. In a chilled mixing bowl, whip the heavy cream, granulated sugar, and vanilla extract until stiff peaks form.
13. Once the cake has cooled, spread the whipped cream over the top of the cake.
14. For the finishing touch, you can optionally sprinkle some cocoa powder or garnish with fresh fruit.
15. Refrigerate the Tres Leches Cake for at least 2 hours, or overnight, to allow the flavors to meld and the cake to become even more moist.

Allow yourself to be transport to the heart of Nicaraguan hospitality, where cherished moments are celebrated with this irresistible treat.

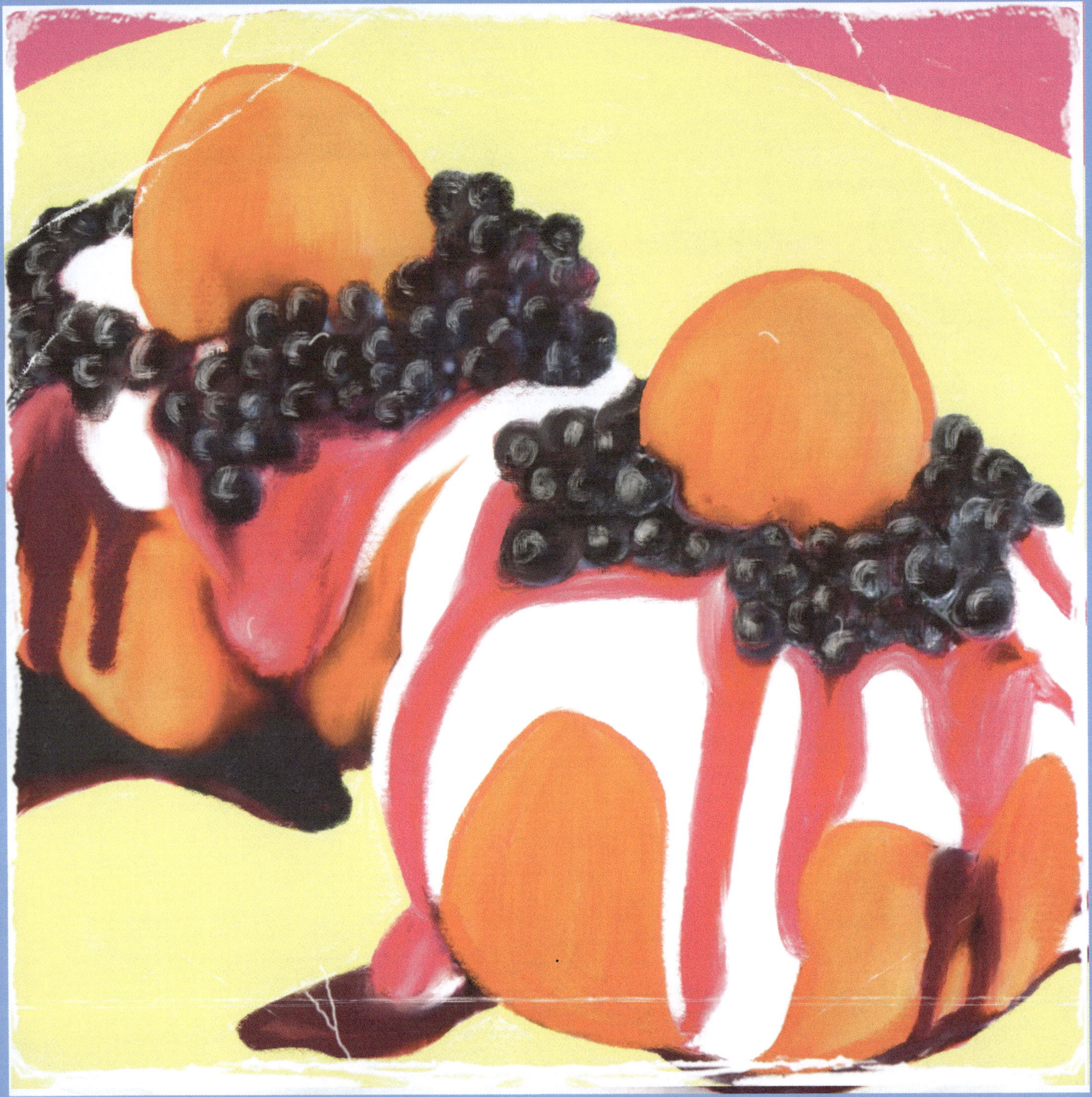

Papanasi

(Romania)

Ingredients:

- 1 1/2 cups cottage cheese
- 1/2 cup all-purpose flour
- 2 tablespoons semolina
- 1/4 cup granulated sugar
- 1 teaspoon vanilla extract
- 1/2 teaspoon baking powder
- Pinch of salt
- Zest of 1 lemon (optional)
- 1 large egg
- Vegetable oil, for frying
- Sour cream, for serving
- Your favorite fruit preserve or jam, for serving

Instructions:

1. In a mixing bowl, combine the cottage cheese, flour, semolina, sugar, vanilla extract, baking powder, salt, and lemon zest (if using). Mix well.
2. Add the egg to the mixture and stir until everything is thoroughly combined, forming a sticky dough.
3. Dust your hands with flour and divide the dough into small portions. Roll each portion into a ball and flatten slightly to form a disk. If the dough is too sticky, add a bit more flour to your hands.
4. In a large frying pan, heat vegetable oil over medium heat. Ensure there is enough oil to submerge the papanasi partially.
5. Gently place the papanasi in the hot oil, being careful not to overcrowd the pan. Fry them until golden brown on both sides, flipping them occasionally. This will take about 4-5 minutes per side.
6. Remove the fried papanasi from the oil and place them on a plate lined with paper towels to absorb excess oil.
7. Serve the papanasi warm, topped with a dollop of sour cream and your favorite fruit preserve or jam.

Indulge in the harmonious pairing of sour cream and sweet fruit preserve, as you immerse yourself in the flavors of Romania.

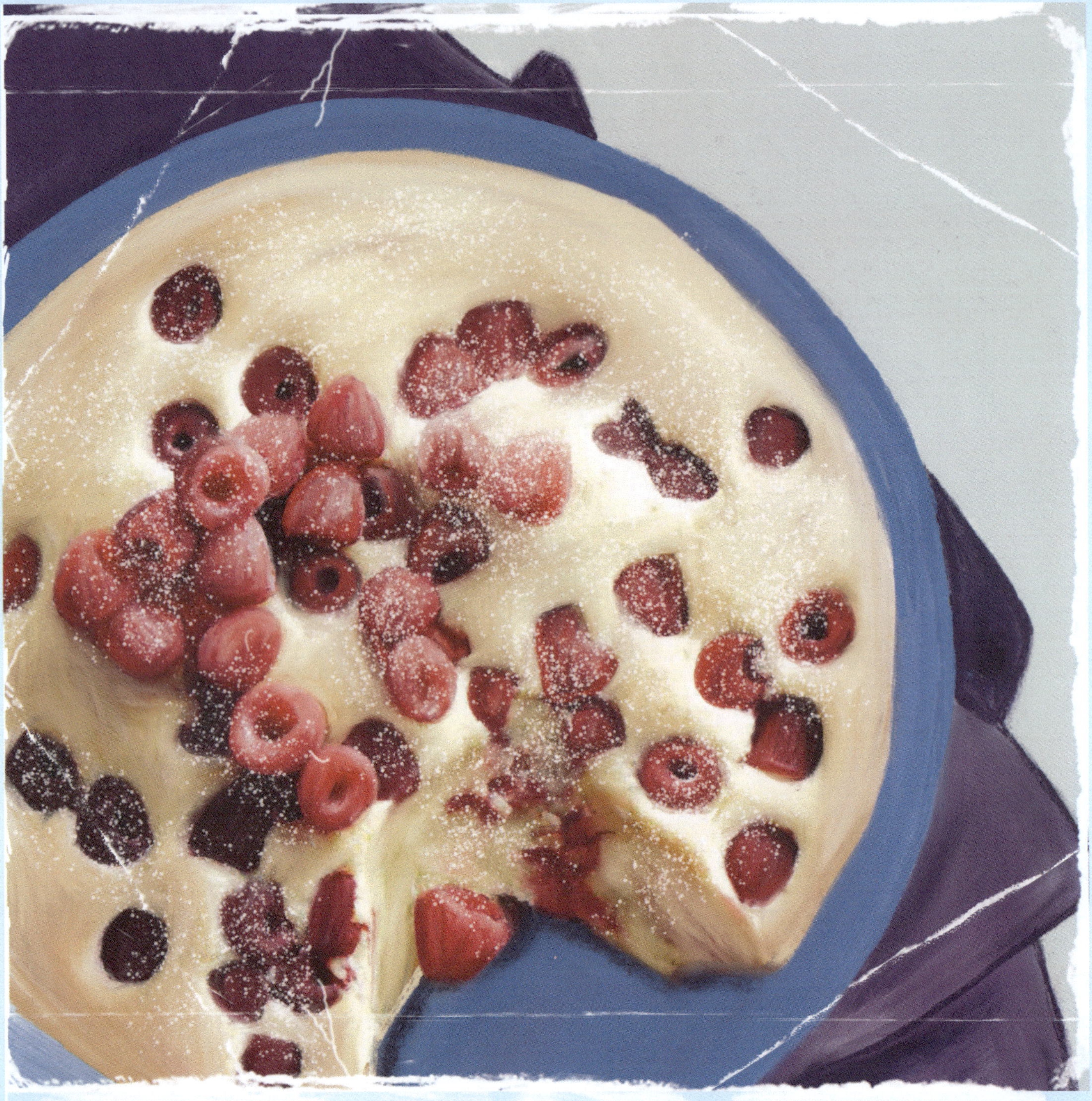

Bublina

(Czech Republic)

Ingredients:

- 2 cups all-purpose flour
- 1 cup granulated sugar
- 1 teaspoon baking powder
- 1/2 teaspoon salt
- 1/2 cup unsalted butter, softened
- 3 large eggs
- 1 cup milk
- 2 cups fresh cherries, pitted
- Powdered sugar, for dusting

Instructions:

1. Preheat your oven to 350°F (175°C). Grease a 9x13-inch baking dish.
2. In a large mixing bowl, combine the flour, sugar, baking powder, and salt.
3. Add the softened butter and eggs to the dry ingredients. Using an electric mixer or a wooden spoon, mix until well combined and the mixture resembles coarse crumbs.
4. Gradually pour in the milk while continuing to mix, until a smooth batter forms.
5. Pour the batter into the greased baking dish, spreading it out evenly.
6. Scatter the pitted cherries over the batter, pressing them lightly into the surface.
7. Bake in the preheated oven for about 30-35 minutes, or until the top is golden brown and a toothpick inserted into the center comes out clean.
8. Remove from the oven and let it cool in the baking dish for a few minutes.
9. Sprinkle powdered sugar generously over the top of the bublanina.
10. Serve the Bublanina warm or at room temperature, sliced into squares or rectangles.

Enjoy this delightful Czech dessert with a cup of tea or coffee, embracing the flavors and traditions of the Czech Republic.

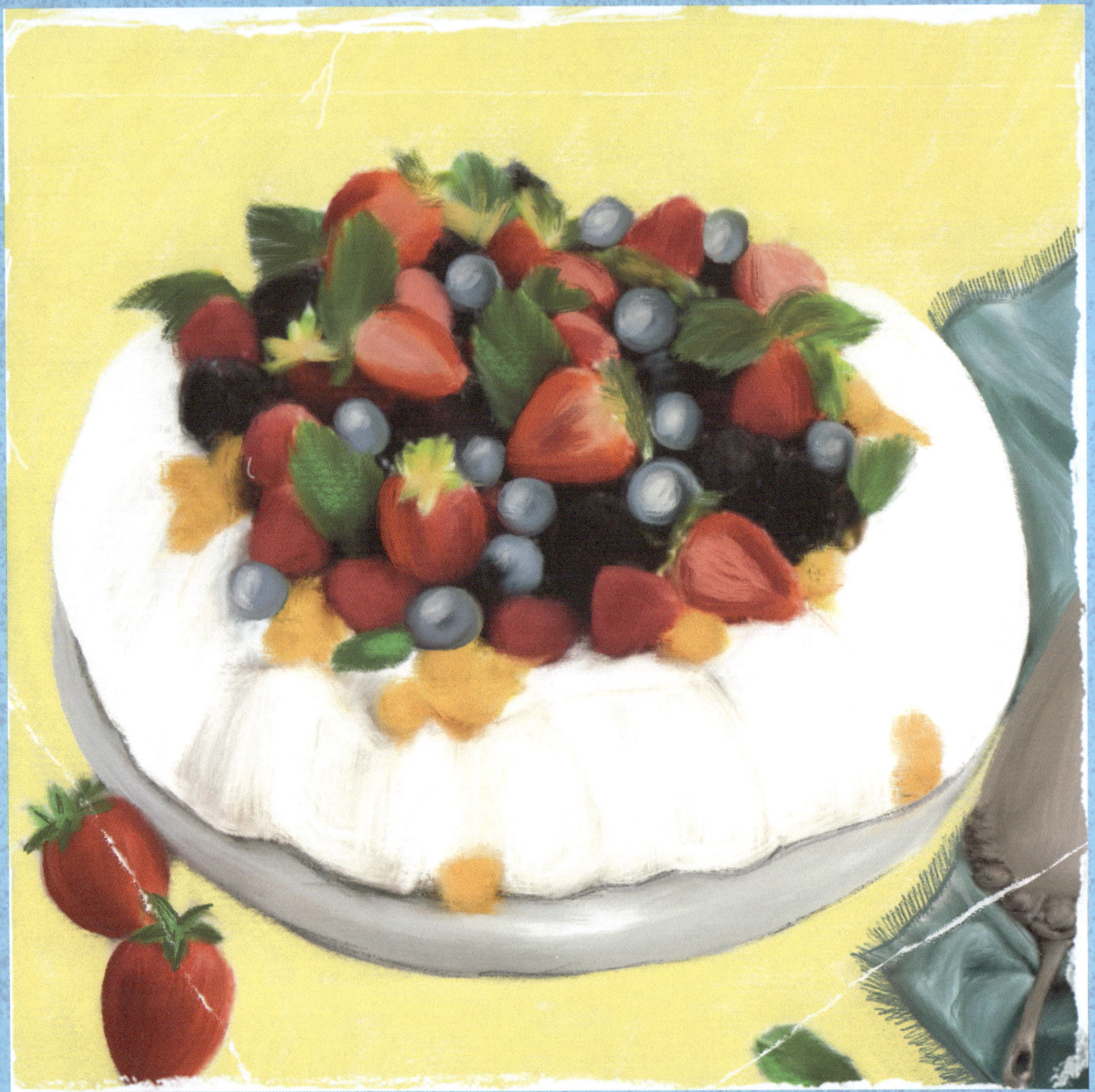

Pavlova

(New Zealand)

Ingredients:
- 4 large egg whites, at room temperature
- 1 cup granulated sugar
- 1 teaspoon white vinegar
- 1 teaspoon cornstarch
- 1 teaspoon vanilla extract
- 1 cup heavy cream
- Fresh fruits (such as berries, kiwi, and passion fruit) for topping

Instructions:

1. Preheat your oven to 300°F (150°C). Line a baking sheet with parchment paper.
2. In a clean, dry mixing bowl, beat the egg whites on medium-high speed until soft peaks form.
3. Gradually add the sugar, a spoonful at a time, while continuing to beat the egg whites. Continue beating until the mixture becomes thick and glossy, and all the sugar has dissolved.
4. In a small bowl, combine the vinegar and cornstarch. Add this mixture to the beaten egg whites, along with the vanilla extract. Gently fold everything together until well combined.
5. Spoon the mixture onto the prepared baking sheet, shaping it into a round or oval shape, forming a slight well in the center to hold the toppings.
6. Place the baking sheet in the preheated oven and immediately reduce the temperature to 250°F (120°C). Bake for about 1 to 1 1/2 hours, or until the pavlova is crisp on the outside and has a light creamy color.
7. Once baked, turn off the oven and let the pavlova cool completely inside the oven with the door slightly ajar. This will help prevent cracking.
8. Just before serving, whip the heavy cream until soft peaks form. Spoon the whipped cream onto the center of the pavlova.
9. Top the pavlova with fresh fruits of your choice, such as berries, kiwi slices, and passion fruit pulp.
10. Serve the pavlova immediately, slicing it into individual portions.

Elevate your dessert repertoire with this exquisite creation that embodies elegance and heavenly delight.

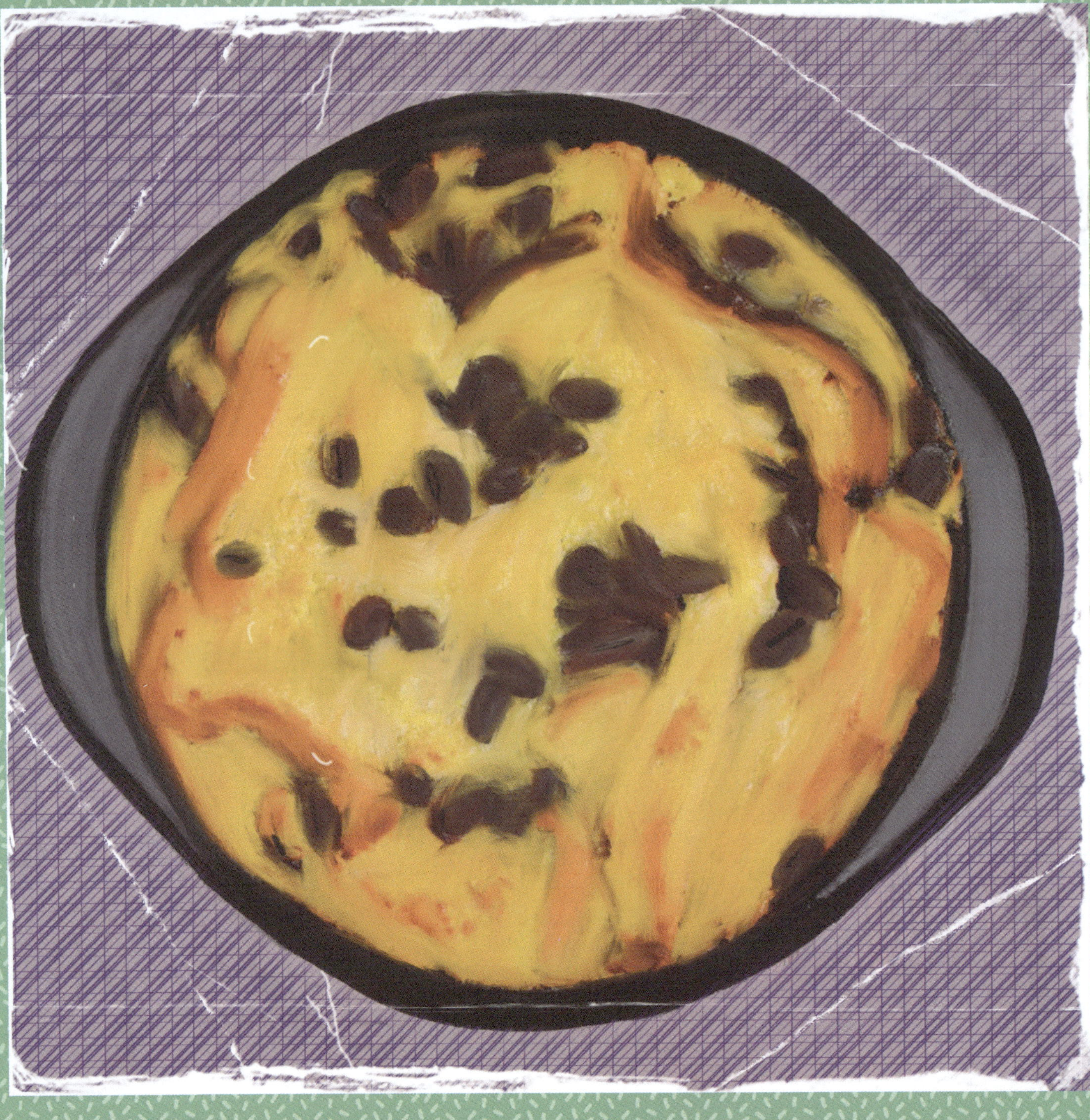

Irish bread pudding

(Ireland)

Ingredients:

- 6 cups day-old bread, cut into cubes (such as Irish soda bread or any crusty bread)
- 2 cups whole milk
- 1 cup heavy cream
- 3/4 cup granulated sugar
- 4 large eggs
- 1 teaspoon vanilla extract
- 1/2 teaspoon ground cinnamon
- 1/4 teaspoon ground nutmeg
- 1/2 cup raisins or currants (optional)
- Butter, for greasing the baking dish
- Whiskey or caramel sauce, for serving (optional)

Instructions:

1. Preheat your oven to 350°F (175°C). Grease a baking dish with butter.
2. Place the bread cubes in the greased baking dish, spreading them out evenly.
3. In a medium saucepan, heat the milk and cream over medium heat until it begins to steam. Remove from heat.
4. In a mixing bowl, whisk together the sugar, eggs, vanilla extract, cinnamon, and nutmeg until well combined.
5. Slowly pour the warm milk and cream mixture into the egg mixture, whisking constantly.
6. If using raisins or currants, sprinkle them over the bread cubes in the baking dish.
7. Pour the custard mixture over the bread cubes, ensuring all the bread is soaked in the liquid.
8. Let the mixture sit for about 15-20 minutes, allowing the bread to absorb the custard.
9. Place the baking dish in the preheated oven and bake for approximately 45-50 minutes, or until the top is golden brown and the custard is set.
10. Remove from the oven and let it cool for a few minutes. Serve warm.
11. For an extra touch, you can drizzle whiskey or caramel sauce over the individual servings before serving.

Enjoy this classic Irish Bread Pudding, a delightful dessert that combines the simplicity of bread with a rich and comforting custard. Its warm and inviting flavors are sure to transport you to the heart of Ireland, making it the perfect treat to enjoy on cozy evenings or as a sweet finale to any meal.

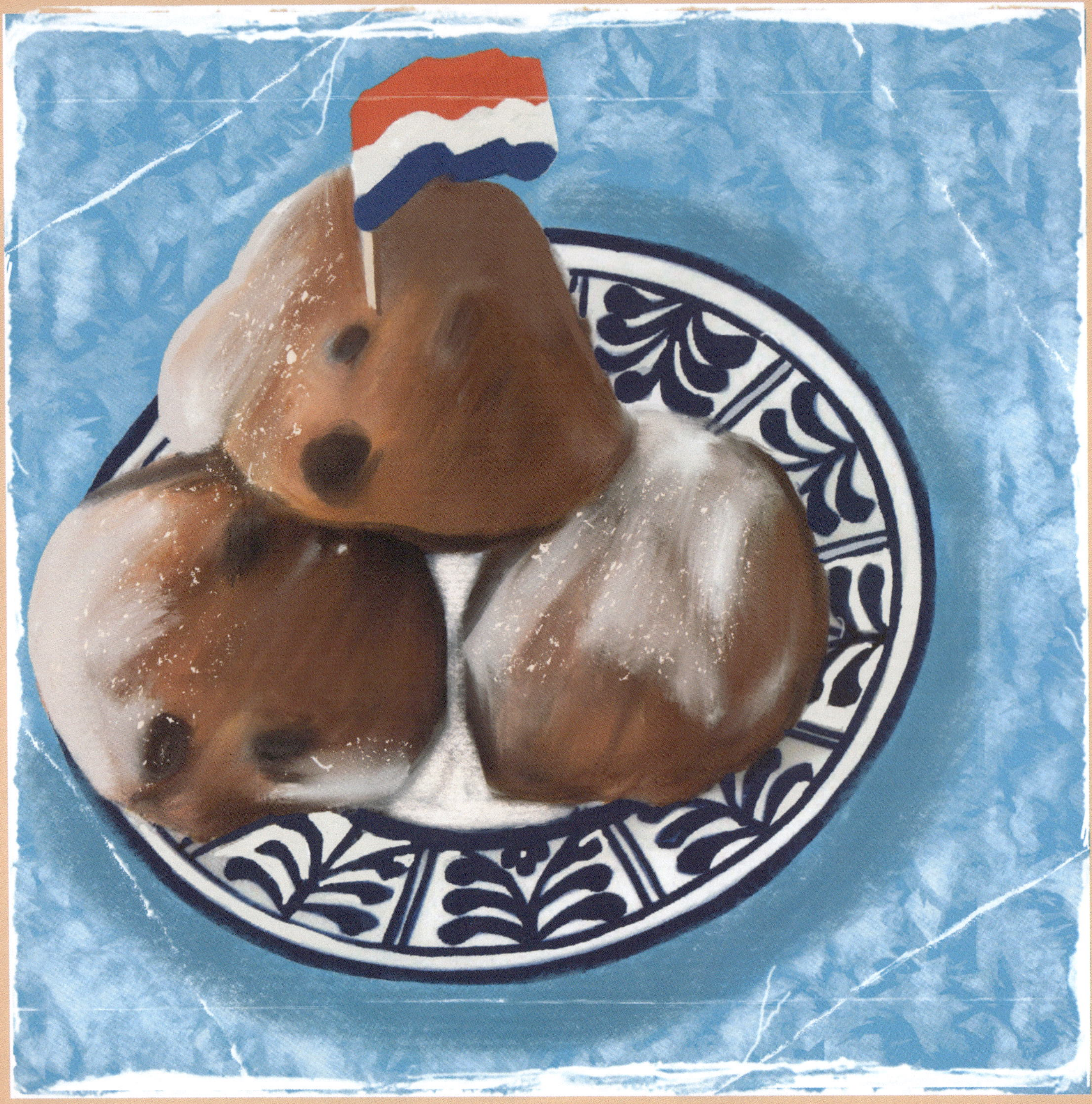

Oliebollen
(Netherlands)

Ingredients:

- 2 ¾ cups all-purpose flour
- 1 ¼ cups lukewarm milk
- 1 ¼ oz (35g) fresh yeast or 2 ½ teaspoons dry yeast
- 1 tablespoon granulated sugar
- 2 eggs
- 1 teaspoon salt
- 1 ½ cups raisins
- Vegetable oil, for frying
- Powdered sugar, for dusting

Instructions:

1. In a large mixing bowl, combine the flour, sugar, and salt. Make a well in the center.
2. In a separate small bowl, crumble the fresh yeast (or sprinkle dry yeast) into the lukewarm milk. Stir until dissolved. Let it sit for a few minutes until frothy.
3. Pour the yeast mixture into the well in the flour mixture. Add the eggs.
4. Stir the ingredients together until well combined and a smooth batter is formed. The batter will be thick and sticky.
5. Cover the bowl with a clean kitchen towel and let the batter rise in a warm place for about 1 hour, or until it has doubled in size.
6. Stir the raisins into the risen batter.
7. In a large, deep pot, heat vegetable oil to a temperature of about 375°F (190°C).
8. Using two spoons or a small ice cream scoop, carefully drop spoonfuls of the batter into the hot oil. Fry them in small batches, turning them occasionally, until golden brown and cooked through. This will take approximately 5-6 minutes per batch.
9. Remove the oliebollen from the oil using a slotted spoon and transfer them to a plate lined with paper towels to drain excess oil.
10. Repeat the frying process with the remaining batter until all the oliebollen are cooked.
11. Once slightly cooled, dust the oliebollen generously with powdered sugar.
12. Serve the Oliebollen warm.

Embrace the whimsical spirit of Dutch tradition with this delectable masterpiece that captures the essence of joyous celebrations.

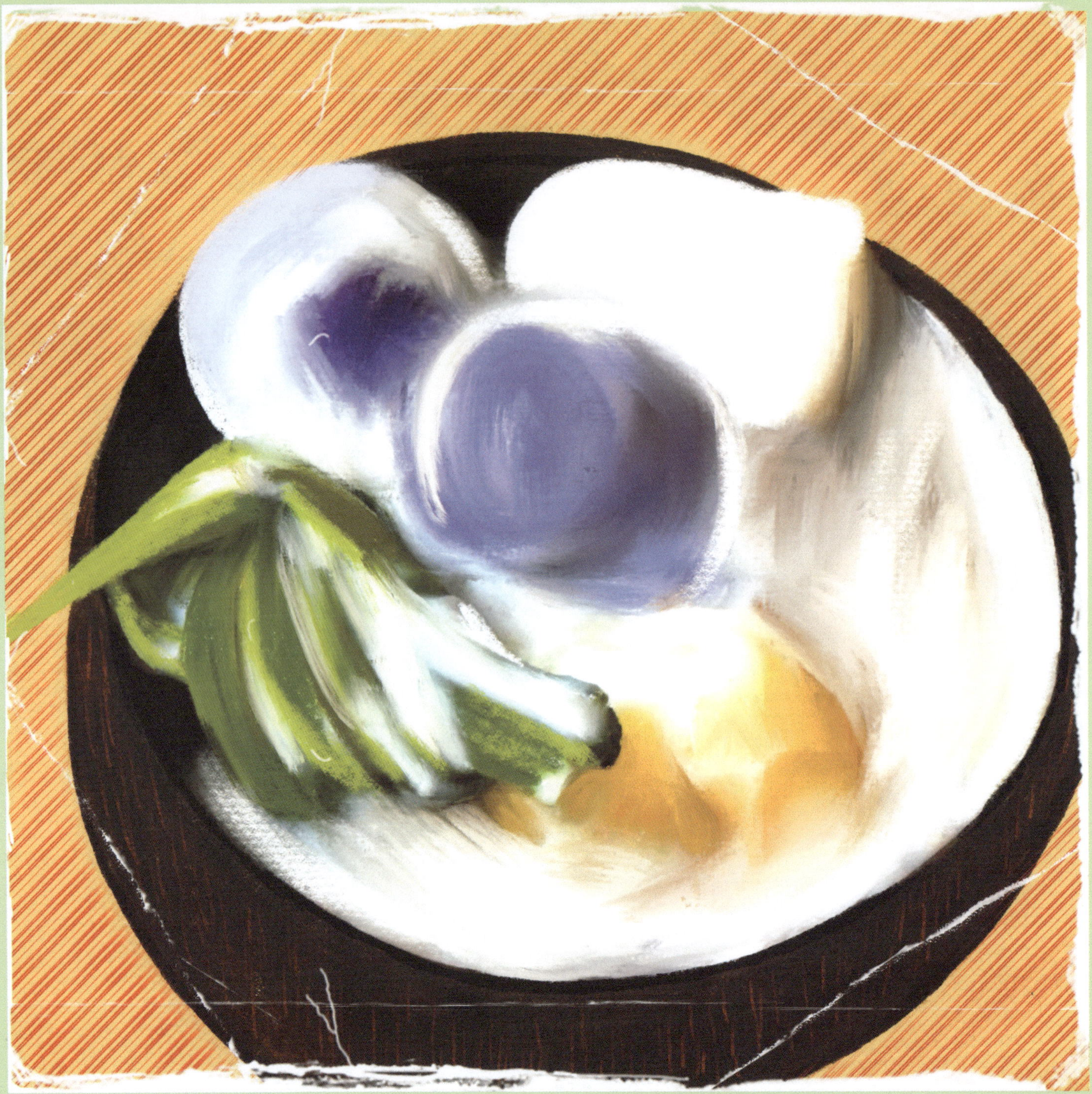

Binignit
(Philippines)

Ingredients:

- 1 cup glutinous rice (malagkit)
- 4 cups water
- 1 cup coconut milk
- 1 cup sweet potato (kamote), peeled and cubed
- 1 cup purple yam (ube), peeled and cubed
- 1 cup ripe jackfruit (langka), sliced
- 1 cup saba bananas, peeled and sliced
- 1 cup tapioca pearls (sago), cooked
- 1 cup palm sugar (latik) or brown sugar
- 1/2 teaspoon vanilla extract
- 1/4 teaspoon salt
- Crushed ice (for serving)

Instructions:

1. In a large pot, combine the glutinous rice and water. Bring to a boil and cook over medium heat until the rice is tender, stirring occasionally. This will take about 20-25 minutes.
2. Add the coconut milk to the pot and stir well. Simmer for another 5 minutes.
3. Add the sweet potato, purple yam, jackfruit, and saba bananas to the pot. Stir gently to mix the ingredients.
4. Continue simmering for about 15-20 minutes, or until the sweet potatoes and yams are tender.
5. Add the cooked tapioca pearls to the pot and stir well.
6. Stir in the palm sugar or brown sugar, vanilla extract, and salt. Adjust the sweetness according to your taste preferences.
7. Continue cooking for another 5 minutes to allow the flavors to meld together.
8. Remove the pot from the heat and let the Binignit cool slightly.
9. Serve the Binignit in bowls, either warm or chilled, depending on your preference.
10. If desired, top each serving with crushed ice to add a refreshing element to the dessert.

With its warm and soothing qualities, Binignit is the perfect treat to savor on special occasions or to enjoy as a chilly day.

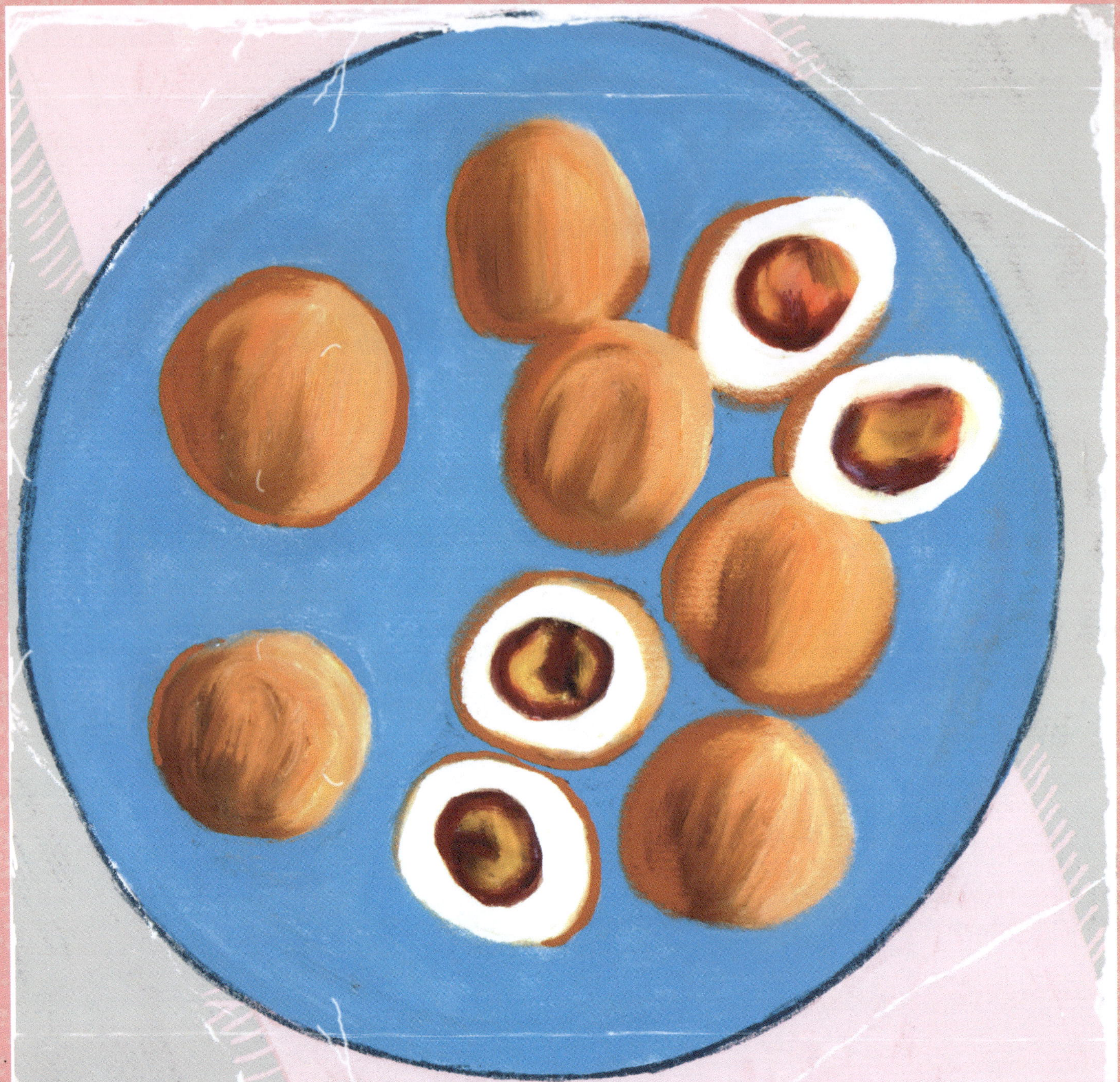

Knedle
(Croatia)

Ingredients:

- 2 cups all-purpose flour
- 1/2 teaspoon baking powder
- Pinch of salt
- 2 tablespoons granulated sugar
- 1/2 cup milk
- 2 tablespoons unsalted butter, melted
- 8 small plums (or other fruit of your choice)
- Cinnamon sugar (for coating)
- Powdered sugar (for garnish)

Instructions:

- In a mixing bowl, whisk together the flour, baking powder, salt, and granulated sugar.
- Add the milk and melted butter to the dry ingredients. Stir until the dough comes together.
- On a lightly floured surface, knead the dough for a few minutes until smooth and elastic.
- Divide the dough into 8 equal portions. Take each portion and flatten it in your hand to form a small disk.
- Take a plum (or other fruit) and remove the pit. Place the fruit in the center of the flattened dough. Carefully wrap the dough around the fruit, sealing it completely.
- Bring a large pot of water to a boil. Gently drop the knedle into the boiling water and cook for about 10-12 minutes, or until they float to the surface. Remove them with a slotted spoon and drain excess water.
- Roll each cooked knedle in the cinnamon sugar mixture until coated.
- Serve the knedle warm, sprinkled with powdered sugar.

Enjoy these delicious Croatian sweet knedle as a delightful dessert! The soft dough wrapped around juicy fruit makes for a delightful treat.

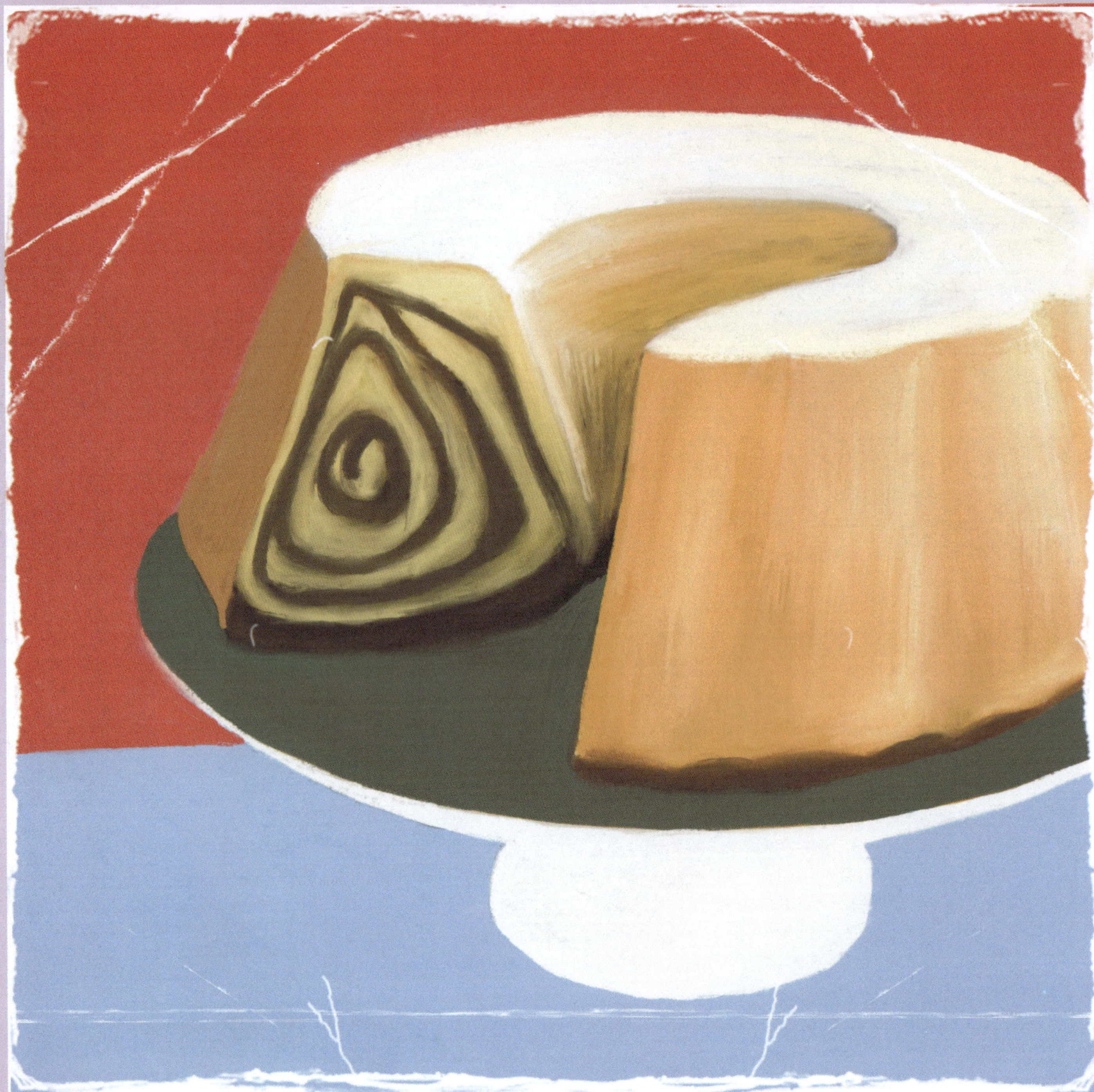

Potica

(Slovenia)

Ingredients:

For the dough:
- 4 cups all-purpose flour
- 1 cup warm milk
- 1/2 cup melted unsalted butter
- 1/4 cup granulated sugar
- 2 tsp active dry yeast
- 1/2 tsp salt
- 2 egg yolks

For the filling:
- 2 cups finely ground walnuts
- 1 cup granulated sugar
- 1/2 cup melted unsalted butter
- 1 cup milk
- 1 tsp vanilla extract
- 1 tsp ground cinnamon

For the brushing:
- 1/4 cup melted unsalted butter

For the dusting:
- Powdered sugar

Instructions:

1. Dissolve 2 tsp sugar and yeast in warm milk. Let it sit for 10 minutes until foamy.
2. In a bowl, mix flour, sugar, and salt. Add melted butter, egg yolks, and yeast mixture. Combine to form a soft dough.
3. Knead the dough for 10-15 minutes. Let it rise for 1-2 hours until doubled in size.
4. In a separate bowl, mix ground walnuts, sugar, melted butter, milk, vanilla extract, and cinnamon for the filling.
5. Roll out the dough into a thin rectangle.
6. Spread the filling evenly on the dough, leaving a small border.
7. Roll the dough tightly into a log.
8. Place the rolled dough in a greased round baking pan.
9. Let the potica rise for 30-45 minutes.
10. Preheat the oven to 350°F (175°C). Brush the top with melted butter.
11. Bake for 45-50 minutes until golden brown.
12. Cool the potica before dusting with powdered sugar.

Indulge in the rich flavors and irresistible charm of traditional Slovene potica, a beloved pastry that weaves together heritage, warmth, and the joy of shared moments around the table.

Glossary

Meringue: A light and airy mixture of beaten egg whites and sugar, often used as a topping or base in desserts. It adds a fluffy and delicate texture to treats like pies, pavlovas, and tarts.

Palm sugar (latik): A natural sweetener made from the sap of certain palm trees, imparting a unique caramel-like flavor to dishes. It adds a hint of richness and complexity to traditional sweets.

Ube: A vibrant purple yam with a subtly sweet and nutty taste, commonly used in Filipino desserts. It lends a gorgeous hue and distinctive flavor to cakes, pastries, and ice creams.

Saba bananas: A variety of bananas with a firm texture and slightly tangy taste, often used in cooking and desserts. They hold their shape well when cooked and provide a natural sweetness to recipes.

Tapioca pearls (sago): Small, translucent balls made from tapioca starch, cooked until they become chewy and gelatinous. They add a delightful texture and can be found in various sweet drinks and puddings.

Glutinous rice (malagkit): A sticky type of rice commonly used in Asian desserts due to its ability to bind ingredients together. It has a chewy texture and absorbs flavors beautifully.

Kamote (sweet potato): A vibrant and sweet root vegetable, frequently used in both savory and sweet dishes. It adds natural sweetness and a smooth, creamy texture to desserts like pies and cakes.

Jackfruit (langka): A tropical fruit with a unique flavor and fragrant aroma, often used as a natural sweetener in desserts. Its sweet and juicy flesh complements a variety of treats.

Purple yam (ube): A root vegetable with a vibrant purple color and subtly sweet flavor. It is a beloved ingredient in Filipino cuisine, adding richness and a lovely hue to traditional sweets.

Evaporated milk: Canned milk with a slightly caramelized flavor, obtained by removing water from fresh milk. It adds a creamy and decadent touch to desserts, custards, and creamy sauces.

Pastry sheets: Thin and flaky sheets of dough commonly used as a base or wrapping for various pastries and desserts. They provide a buttery and crisp texture to treats like turnovers, strudels, and pies.

Caster sugar: Also known as superfine sugar, it is a finely ground sugar with a texture between granulated sugar and powdered sugar. It dissolves quickly and easily, making it ideal for recipes where a smoother texture is desired, such as meringues, whipped creams, and delicate cakes.

Custard powder: A convenient mixture of cornstarch, vanilla flavoring, and yellow food coloring used to make custard-based desserts. It simplifies the process of creating a smooth and creamy custard, which can be enjoyed on its own or incorporated into other desserts.

Cooking terms

Bake: Cook food in an oven using dry heat, creating a delicious golden exterior and ensuring even cooking throughout.

Blanch: Briefly cook food, typically vegetables or fruits, in boiling water and then quickly transfer them to ice water. This technique helps preserve color, texture, and nutrients.

Boil: Cook food in a liquid at a high temperature until large bubbles vigorously break the surface. It is often used for rapidly cooking pasta, grains, or vegetables.

Broil: Cook food under high direct heat, usually in the oven or broiler, for a short time to achieve a caramelized and slightly charred surface.

Caramelize: Cook food with sugar so that it is coated with caramel.

Coat: Cover something with a wet or dry substance, for example with a layer of butter.

Crimp: The process of pressing together the side and top crusts of a pie, usually by pinching the pastry together in a fluted pattern.

Dust: The process of sprinkling a thin layer of powdered ingredient such as cocoa powder, flour and confectioners' sugar over food.

Fold: Gently combine ingredients, especially light and airy mixtures, by using a spatula or spoon to cut vertically through the mixture and then gently turn it over. This method helps maintain the airy texture.

Glaze: Coat a food with sugar, a sugar syrup, or some other glossy, edible substance.

Grate: Shred food into small pieces using a grater or shredder, perfect for adding texture or incorporating ingredients like cheese or vegetables.

Sauté: Gently cook food in a small amount of oil or fat over high heat, stirring or tossing the ingredients until they are lightly browned and aromatic.

Season: Enhance the flavor of food by adding the right amount of salt, pepper, herbs, or spices. Proper seasoning is key to achieving a well-balanced and delicious dish.

Simmer: Cook food slowly in liquid over low heat, maintaining a gentle bubbling or simmering action. This method ensures even cooking and allows flavors to meld together.

Steam: Cook food by placing it above or in a small amount of boiling water. This gentle and moist cooking method helps retain the food's natural flavors and nutrients.

✨ Fascinating facts ✨

Tarte aux Fraises: a classic strawberry tart ibelieved to have originated in the late 19th century during he Belle Époque, a period known for its elegance and sophistication in France. It quickly became a beloved dessert, especially during the spring and summer months when fresh strawberries are abundant. The combination of the buttery tart shell, luscious whipped cream, and juicy strawberries creates a delightful balance of flavors and textures that has stood the test of time.

Bingka Ubi: a beloved dessert in Southeast Asia with a rich history that traces back centuries. The name "bingka" is derived from the Malay language, meaning "cake," while "ubi" refers to the key ingredient, cassava. This delectable cake has its roots in the region's diverse culinary heritage, influenced by indigenous cultures and the colonial history of Southeast Asia. Traditionally, Bingka Ubi was prepared during special occasions and festive celebrations, where families would gather to enjoy its delightful flavors.

Knafeh: An iconic dessert in Lebanon as well in many other Middle Eastern countries, a symbol of hospitality and celebration. It is often served during festive occasions, weddings, and family gatherings. Its origins can be traced back to the city of Nablus in Palestine, where it is believed to have originated during the Ottoman era. While the traditional version of Knafeh features a sweet cheese filling, there are various regional variations that showcase different fillings and toppings. Some versions incorporate clotted cream, others use a semolina-based custard, and some even feature a combination of nuts and honey.

Black Forest Cake: a classic and internationally renowned dessert that originated in the Black Forest region of Germany. This iconic cake is named after the region known for its dense forests, charming villages, and the production of a famous cherry liqueur called kirsch. Legend has it that the cake was inspired by the traditional costume of the Black Forest region, with the dark chocolate representing the traditional black attire, the cream symbolising the white shirt, and the cherries signifying the red pompoms worn on the costumes.

Esterházy torta: a renowned Hungarian dessert that carries a rich history and a regal association. This elegant cake was named after the influential Esterházy family, who were prominent nobles and patrons of the arts in Hungary. The cake consists of multiple layers of thin almond meringue or sponge cake, which are filled with a luscious buttercream made with ground walnuts or hazelnuts. The pattern is often reminiscent of the Esterházy family's coat of arms, with its intricate and elegant design.

Lamingtons: iconic Australian treats believed to have been invented in the late 19th century by a maid-servant to Lord Lamington, who was the Governor of Queensland at the time. The story goes that the maid-servant was tasked with making a sponge cake for unexpected guests. With limited ingredients at hand, she improvised by cutting the leftover sponge cake into squares, dipping them in chocolate sauce, and rolling them in coconut to avoid getting messy hands. The result was a delectable treat that impressed Lord Lamington and became an instant hit. What started as a humble creation in the Lamington household soon gained popularity across Australia. Today, Lamingtons are considered a quintessential Australian dessert, enjoyed at picnics, afternoon teas, and special occasions. They even have their own national day of celebration on July 21st, known as National Lamington Day.

Bastani Sonnati: a beloved for centuries Iranian dessert often enjoyed during special occasions and celebrations, including weddings and festive gatherings. In Persian culture, it symbolizes joy, abundance, and hospitality, making it a delightful treat to share with loved ones. Bastani Sonnati is commonly served in various ways, including scooped into cones, presented in bowls, or even sandwiched between delicate wafers. It is often garnished with pistachios, almonds, or other nuts to add a delightful crunch and enhance the overall experience.

Fudge: an American sweet treat believed to have its roots in the late 19th century. One fascinating theory suggests that the invention of fudge was actually a result of a failed caramel-making attempt. The story goes that a batch of caramel was accidentally cooked for too long or at the wrong temperature, resulting in a grainy texture. However, rather than discarding the failed caramel, resourceful confectioners decided to embrace its unique texture and taste, and thus, fudge was born. The name "fudge" itself is said to have an interesting origin as well. It is believed to have originated from the phrase "fudged up," which was a colloquial term used to describe a mistake or mishap. This ties back to the accidental creation of fudge, as it was essentially a "fudged up" version of caramel. Over time, the name stuck and became associated specifically with the delightful confection we know today.

Empire biscuits: a delightful treat that is both sweet and buttery. Its origin can be traced back to the Victorian era in Scotland. The name "Empire" is said to have been inspired by the British Empire, reflecting the influence of British colonialism during that time. In Scotland, Empire biscuits are commonly served during tea time or as a special treat on festive occasions such as weddings, birthdays, and holidays.

Carac: a pastry from Switzerland that has earned its place among the country's beloved sweet treats. It is typically made from a rich, flaky pastry dough and filled with a smooth and creamy chocolate ganache or buttercream. The name "Carac" is derived from the French word "escargot," which means snail. This is because the pastry is often shaped like a snail, with a spiral design, reminiscent of the shell.

Pastel de Nata: also known as Portuguese custard tart, originated in the early 19th century in Lisbon, Portugal. It was created by Catholic monks who resided in the Jerónimos Monastery. The monks used egg whites to starch their clothing, leaving behind a surplus of egg yolks. In their resourcefulness, they developed a recipe that utilized these excess egg yolks, resulting in the birth of Pastel de Nata. One fascinating aspect of Pastel de Nata is its connection to the iconic Belém district in Lisbon. The recipe was initially kept a secret by the monks, who baked and sold the pastries exclusively to sustain themselves. However, in the early 1830s, following the liberal revolution in Portugal, the monastery was closed and the recipe was sold to a nearby sugar refinery, now known as the famous Pastéis de Belém. To this day, the Pastéis de Belém bakery continues to produce Pastel de Nata using the original secret recipe, delighting locals and visitors alike.

Malabi: a creamy, chilled pudding-like dessert that has its roots in Middle Eastern cuisine. It is believed to have originated in ancient Persia and then spread throughout the region, including Israel. The name "Malabi" is derived from the Arabic word "muhallabia," which means "milk pudding." Malabi is commonly enjoyed during festive occasions, such as Ramadan or other special celebrations, as well as a refreshing dessert on hot summer days. It has also become a popular street food dessert in Israel, with stalls and vendors offering their own unique twists and flavor variations. While the basic recipe remains consistent, different regions and cultures within Israel may add their own distinct touches to Malabi, such as using different spices, incorporating fruit purees, or experimenting with alternative toppings.

Pastelitos de Guayaba: a delightful treat that originates from Cuba and holds a special place in Cuban cuisine. The term "Pastelitos" translates to "little pastries" in Spanish, reflecting their small, individual size. The word "Guayaba" refers to guava, the key ingredient that gives these pastries their distinct flavor and character. One fascinating aspect of Pastelitos de Guayaba is their connection to Cuban culture and tradition. These pastries are commonly enjoyed during special occasions and celebrations, such as birthdays, holidays, and family gatherings. They are also a popular treat for breakfast or enjoyed as an afternoon snack with a cup of coffee.

Merengón: a dessert which holds a special place in Colombian culinary history and culture. It is said to have originated in the city of Cali, which is often referred to as the "salsa capital" of Colombia. Merengón is believed to have been inspired by the popular Caribbean dessert known as "Merengue," which features a similar meringue base. However, Colombians added their unique twist by incorporating an abundant array of tropical fruits that are native to the region. The dessert gained popularity throughout Colombia and became a beloved treat, especially during celebrations and festivals. It is often associated with joyful occasions such as weddings, birthdays, and holidays. In fact, Merengón is frequently prepared and enjoyed during the famous Cali Fair, a week-long celebration of music, dance, and gastronomy that attracts visitors from all over the world.

Tres Leches Cake: a beloved treat which is not only enjoyed as a dessert for special occasions or celebrations but is also commonly savored as an everyday treat. The cake's name, "Tres Leches," translates to "Three Milks" in English, referring to its signature ingredient combination. The cake is soaked in a mixture of three different types of milk—evaporated milk, condensed milk, and whole milk—after baking. This soaking process gives the cake its distinctive moist and tender texture and infuses it with rich, creamy flavors.

Papanasi: a beloved Romanian dessert believed to have been enjoyed for centuries. The name "Papanasi" is derived from the Romanian word "papa," meaning "to eat," and the suffix "-nasi," which is a term of endearment. Together, they create a playful and affectionate name for this delightful treat, which is also often enjoyed as a dessert during festive occasions, family gatherings, and even as a comforting treat on a cozy evening. It is a dessert that brings people together, evoking feelings of nostalgia and celebration.

Bublina: a delightful Czech dessert that holds a special place in Czech culinary traditions and becomes a popular treat to share during gatherings, picnics, or celebrations. It is often enjoyed alongside a cup of coffee or tea, creating a cozy and welcoming atmosphere. The tradition of sharing Bublina reflects the Czech culture's emphasis on hospitality, generosity, and the importance of building and maintaining relationships. An interesting fact about the name of this sweet delight is that "Bublina" in Czech translates to "bubble". The name is derived from the appearance of the dessert, which is often studded with juicy fruits on the surface, resembling bubbles.

Pavlova: a a meringue-based dessert that is believed to have originated in either Australia or New Zealand. However, the exact origin of Pavlova has been a topic of debate between these two countries for many years. The dessert was named after the renowned Russian ballerina Anna Pavlova, who toured both Australia and New Zealand in the 1920s. Legend has it that Pavlova's ethereal and delicate dancing inspired the creation of this light and airy dessert, which mimics her grace and elegance.

Irish bread pudding: a classic Irish dessert that has its roots in frugality and resourcefulness. In Ireland, bread was traditionally a staple food, and it was essential not to let any go to waste. The dessert emerged as a clever way to use up stale or leftover bread. The pudding is often associated with family gatherings, holidays, and special occasions. It is a dessert that evokes a sense of nostalgia and reminds people of cherished moments shared around the table with loved ones.

Oliebollen: a traditional Dutch treat enjoyed during the festive season, particularly on New Year's Eve. They are deep-fried dough balls that have a crispy and golden exterior and a soft, fluffy interior. The history of oliebollen dates back centuries in the Netherlands. It is believed that they were first made in the 17th century during the Dutch Golden Age. Oliebollen were initially associated with the pagan festival of Yule, which celebrated the winter solstice. Over time, they became closely linked to the Christmas and New Year's celebrations in Dutch culture. The preparation of oliebollen involves making a yeast-based dough that is typically enriched with ingredients such as milk, flour, eggs, sugar, and sometimes raisins or currants. The dough is then left to rise, allowing the yeast to ferment and create air pockets, resulting in a light and fluffy texture. Traditionally, oliebollen were cooked in hot oil in large cast-iron cauldrons, giving them their distinctive round shape. The dough balls are carefully dropped into the hot oil and fried until they turn a beautiful golden brown. They are then dusted with powdered sugar, giving them a sweet and irresistible coating.

Binignit: a traditional Filipino dessert often prepared and shared during religious festivals and celebrations, such as Holy Week and All Saints' Day. The dessert brings people together and signifies the spirit of togetherness and gratitude for the bountiful harvest and blessings.

Knedle: a beloved and iconic dish in Croatian cuisine, appreciated for their soft and pillowy texture and delightful fillings.While knedle are commonly associated with sweet fillings such as plums, apricots, or strawberries, they can also be made with savory fillings, offering a unique twist on this traditional dish. Knedle have their roots in Central European cuisine and are believed to have originated in the broader region of Austria-Hungary, which encompassed present-day Croatia. The name "knedle" is derived from the German word "Knödel," which means "dumpling." This German influence is attributed to the historical and cultural ties between the two regions.

Potica: a traditional Slovenian dessert that has been enjoyed in Slovenia for generations and is often associated with special occasions and festive celebrations. It has become an iconic symbol of Slovenian culinary heritage. The word "potica" itself has an interesting origin. It is derived from the Slovenian verb "zviti," meaning "to roll" or "to twist." This refers to the distinctive preparation method of rolling a thin layer of sweet dough around a flavorful filling, creating a spiral-shaped cake. The making of Potica is a labor of love and often involves intricate techniques passed down through generations. The dough is rolled out thinly, and the filling is evenly spread, creating layers of flavor. It is then carefully rolled into a cylindrical shape and baked to perfection, resulting in a beautifully swirled cake. In recognition of its cultural significance, Potica was included on the UNESCO Representative List of the Intangible Cultural Heritage of Humanity in 2019. This acknowledgment highlights the cultural value and importance of Potica in Slovenian society and its enduring legacy as a beloved dessert.

My recipes

My recipes

My recipes

My recipes